Forging the Path:
Fifteen Years of Volunteer Support For Virginia's Parks

Preface by Joe Elton
Director, Virginia State Parks

Printed in the United States of America
ISBN: 9781482042115

For all general information, please contact:
Virginia Association for Parks (VAFP)
3601 Burton Road
Bumpass, VA 23024

virginiaparks.org

Photographs in this book are credited to:
Virginia Department of Conservation and Recreation
Virginia Association for Parks
Various Friends Groups of Virginia State Parks
National Park Service
Various Friends Groups of National Parks

VAFP members tour Natural Tunnel State Park in the fall of 2011

CONTENTS

Preface

During the dark days of the American Civil War, President Abraham Lincoln and the United States Congress passed an act to protect the Yosemite Valley by making it a state park. In 1890, Yosemite became a national park, thus making Niagara Falls America's oldest state park. The scenic attraction was born from the New York State budget of 1885.

Stephen T. Mather was successful in creating the National Park Service in 1916

Stephen T. Mather

with the goal of preserving America's most remarkable and iconic landscapes. In the process, he understood that the federal government couldn't do it all.

Mather knew there would be political pressure to make many less iconic sites national parks. He combated that pressure by hosting National Conferences on State Parks starting in 1921. Those conferences helped the nation firmly establish the state park idea. Essentially, they defined a state park as a close-to-home outdoor recreation venue that showcases remarkable examples of the state's diverse natural beauty.

Virginia governors beginning with E. Lee Trinkle (1922-1926), Harry F. Byrd (1926-1930), John Garland Pollard (1930-1934), and George C. Peery (1934-1938) were instrumental in planting the seed and nurturing the idea of a Virginia state park system.

E. Lee Trinkle

William E. Carson became the first chairman of the Virginia Commission on Conservation and Development in 1926 and began a campaign to sell Virginians on the value of creating a state park system. He said in 1933, following a meeting

William E. Carson

with President Franklin D. Roosevelt when the president agreed to bring Civilian Conservation Corps Camps to Virginia for the express purpose of building state parks, that *"this (Great Depression Recovery Program) is the chance of a lifetime."*

Harry F. Byrd

Carson did not have the first acre of land, nor did he have money for the first acre of land to make this depression-era dream come true. What he did have was a dream and the power of persuasion. Carson began at once to sell his ideas and promote Roosevelt's offer to provide the money and manpower to build parks, if only Virginia could provide the land. Philanthropy played a huge role.

John G. Pollard

George C. Peery

Carson succeeded in convincing the Douthat Land Company, the Lincoln brothers of Marion, Junius B. Fishburn of Roanoke, and a Norfolk syndicate to donate land for Douthat, Hungry Mother, Fairy Stone, and Seashore State Parks. Then he asked the General Assembly to provide funding for land between the ancestral birthplaces of Robert E. Lee (Stratford Hall) and George Washington (Wakefield) for a park on the Potomac River in Westmoreland County, named Westmoreland State Park, and land at the confluence of the Dan and Staunton Rivers for Staunton River State Park. Before he was done, he had assembled the land and organized the partnerships with the federal government to build six state parks (Seashore, Staunton River, Westmoreland, Fairy Stone, Douthat, and Hungry Mother).

On June 15, 1936, Governor George C. Peery stood on a stage at Hungry Mother State Park, and with some 5,000 listening to his remarks, said *"Our new state park system has been built to serve the working man. The working man is entitled to more than a bare existence, and so it is the duty of government, either state or national, to help bring to him some of the pleasures the world has to offer. The state parks are for all the people, and not only will they afford recreation for our own people, but will attract tourists from other states. A movement of this kind is the answer to those who argue that we are going backward. There is no place for Communism, Nazism or Fascism in this country; but there must be recreational opportunities available to the rich and poor alike. I believe these parks will contribute greatly to the national good as we go forward to the splendid destiny that awaits in the future."*

The first 75 years of Virginia State Parks is about good planning, smart public relations, vision, and dedication. It is also about always present societal and economic struggles, the Great Depression, Segregation, Civil Rights, and all the bust and boom through-out the decades.

In 1936, more than 90,000 park visits were reported up line to Richmond; what an impressive beginning! Could they have dreamt that 75 years later what began as a system of six parks would become an expanded system of 35 state parks with more than 8 million annual visits?

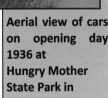

Aerial view of cars on opening day 1936 at Hungry Mother State Park in Marion, Virginia

Development of Virginia State Parks

1926-Gov. Byrd established the State Commission on Conservation and Development
1929-The Virginia Academy of Science, the Garden Club of Virginia and the Izaak Walton League met in Richmond to discuss the need for state parks.
1929-What Carson called a *"skeleton organization,"* known as the Landscape Division headed by Robin (R.E.) Burson, was established to find suitable locations for park development.
1931-Seashore State Park Association, a citizens' group, traveled with Burson to the National Conference on State Parks, which gave them a "broader vision of the real value of state parks." (continued)

As of 2012, only six men have served as Virginia's state parks director.

- R. E. Burson (1936-1939), followed by his assistant ;
- Randolph O'Dell (1939-1961), followed by his assistant ;
- Ben Bolen (1961-1981), followed by his assistant ;
- Ronald D. Sutton (1982-1991), followed by his assistant ;
- Dennis Baker (1991-1994) followed by;
- Joe Elton (1994-present), who broke the string of assistants becoming state parks directors. This short chain of individuals, with relatively long service, has provided an opportunity for each to make his mark on our state park system. Along the way, they led the development of a system of state parks that has been recognized nationally for excellence in parks and recreation management.

Park Directors, left to right: Ben Bolen, Ron Sutton, Joe Elton, Dennis Baker, pictured with their Administrative Assistant, Barbara Jackson

Photos of CCC members building the first six Virginia State Parks. The CCC was responsible for building national, state, and local park facilities across the United States.

1932-Virginia hosted the conference at Cape Henry's dunes. That same year, Burson was appointed "Associate Supervisor" of parks.
1933-Depression led President Roosevelt to create the Civilian Conservation Corps (CCC) to put young men to work in forests and parks.
1933-Carson hosted President Roosevelt at Camp Rapidan (Hoover) near Shenandoah National Park. Carson proposed using the CCC to develop a system of state parks.
1933-Camp Carson, first CCC, at Douthat State Park. In the following months, camps established on other acquired park land.
1936-June 15, the first six state parks were opened in Virginia.

By 1994 Virginia government was appreciating the value and need for citizen volunteers more than ever, and the Department of Conservation and Recreation created a short-lived new section, the Division of Volunteerism and Constituent Services (1994-1997). This emphasis on volunteerism influenced state parks to devote more time and attention to the development of Friends groups. When Vera Guise and Robert Williams approached me about working with them to develop a statewide organization to promote volunteerism on public lands, it seemed like a worthy idea. I recall a number of phone conversations and planning discussions that preceded the first statewide meeting in November of 1997 at what was then a Sheraton Hotel near Fredericksburg. I was invited to be the dinner speaker and I believed my role was to encourage them and thank them for their efforts to help public land agencies recruit, train, and nurture volunteers – for the benefit they can provide parks, but also for the health and well being benefits that volunteering provides the volunteer.

Vera Guise left to work with the National Parks Conservation Association, but it was clear to me that Robert Williams had the passion and desire to institutionalize their efforts by forming an association with a mission to boost state and national parks.

Robert Williams

How could I have known that this weekend in 1997 and the inspirational speaker's gift would mark the beginning of a 15 year partnership? How could I have known there would be so many success stories? Who could have predicted a robust volunteer program that generates more than 340,000 hours and 6,000 volunteers a year? Or the millions of dollars raised for projects benefiting every age visitor-from toddler playgrounds to fitness trails used for senior citizen physical therapy? New technology tools, modern websites, virtual storytellers, touch screen information kiosks, events, festivals, concerts, and many other programs have all been made possible by harnessing the creative and selfless power of citizen volunteers.

In this historical account, you will learn how it happened, who provided leadership, and more specifically, what has been achieved in terms of advocacy, volunteerism, and fundraising. The deep recesses of many minds, old files and searchable databases have been harvested to provide the most accurate account of the history of the Virginia Association for Parks. It is a remarkable story, and one would think we could all remember what started 15 years ago and what has happened in the ensuing years. Not so. We all turn the page and begin each day with new challenges, new projects, and new mountains to climb. So my hat is off to all who have

Jo and Johnny Finch

helped capture the remarkable success story of this still teenaged organization. Among those involved, I must take the liberty of singling out three for special recognition. I've been fond of saying Robert Williams was the inspired founder of VAFP – but it was Johnny and Jo Finch who breathed life into it and gave it a soul.

I dedicate this Preface to these inspirational leaders and loyal friends of Virginia State Parks. May their example inspire other leaders to follow in their footsteps.

Introduction

The Virginia Association for Parks (VAFP) is unique. Based on information gathered from the National Association of State Park Directors and other national organizations related to park conservation, VAFP was the first group in America to attempt to create one statewide umbrella organization with the mission to support a statewide system of parks regardless of which government (local, state, or federal) has jurisdiction over the park. A major component, and necessary early step, of this mission was to provide assistance in forming new park support organizations, usually called "Friends" groups, for those parks that did not already have one, and to provide training and other technical assistance to new and existing Friends groups to build their organizational capacity so they can better serve their individual parks.

Johnny Finch and Joe Elton

This book is just a brief history of the Virginia Association for Parks. Rather than provide a detailed description of every action and every effort of the Association over the past 15 years, which would not be possible to cover in a book this size, the authors have selected highlights that tell the story of the Association's successes. It is also the hope of VAFP that this book may help encourage and serve as an instructional guide to citizens interested in starting Park Friends Groups or similar umbrella groups in other states.

The Formative Years (1997 - 2002)

The Vision

"Never doubt that a small group of thoughtful, committed citizens can change the world. Indeed, it is the only thing that ever has." Although this famous quote by Margaret Mead was never the official credo of the Virginia Association for Parks, the philosophy behind the quote was certainly an encouragement and guiding principle of the organization from its founding.

In 1997, Vera Guise, President of American Grassroots, realized that far more could be accomplished for individual parks within a state if small park support groups worked together rather than working individually. Her desire was to see an organization that would support all parks in the state regardless of what government (local, state, or federal) had jurisdiction over the park. Her vision was to establish an umbrella

Douthat State Park

organization that could accomplish two major goals: first to help establish local support organizations for specific parks, typically called Friends groups, and second, to serve a coordinating role to encourage these Friends groups to work for the greater good of the overall park system.

After formulating her plan, Vera decided to test her theory. Although she lived in North Carolina and had served as the executive director of Friends of the Blue Ridge Parkway, Vera decided to use Virginia as a test pilot. She identified park leaders in Virginia and began to discuss her ideas with them. When she shared her dream with Marty Leicester, Superintendent of Fredericksburg and Spotsylvania National Military Park, Marty said she knew someone who might be willing to help Vera bring her plan to fruition.

First Statewide Conference

In the summer of 1997, Marty Leicester invited Vera Guise to Fredericksburg to meet with Robert Williams, who had founded two support organizations for Fredericksburg and Spotsylvania National Military Park: Friends of Wilderness Battlefield and Friends of Fredericksburg Area Battlefields. Robert also represented Fredericksburg and Spotsylvania National Military Park on the National Parks Mid-Atlantic Council.

Robert was honored to have the opportunity to help with Vera's vision and agreed to host a statewide park conference in Fredericksburg that November. Vera was able to recruit Sarah Bishop of Partners in Parks to assist with the effort. Vera also frequently consulted with Lynn Davis, a long-time park advocate who was an instrumental leader in the Friends of the Blue Ridge Parkway. While Vera and Sarah prepared the overall program and identified trainers, Robert coordinated the local logistics for the conference, secured funding, and invited the keynote speaker for the event: Joe Elton, Director of Virginia State Parks. Funding for the conference came from

the National Park Service Northeast Region, the National Parks Conservation Association, the National Park Trust, the National Parks Mid-Atlantic Council, and Friends of Fredericksburg Area Battlefields.

From November 7 to 9, 1997, citizen park leaders from all over Virginia, park officials representing state and national parks, and others from key regional and national agencies and organizations gathered at the Fredericksburg Sheraton to learn, share, and plan for the future of Virginia's parks. The conference theme was *Friends and Partners for Virginia's Parks*. Training sessions included *Friends – A Park's Other Natural Resource; Partnership Agreements; Growing Members and Donors; Advocacy: Promoting Your Park;* and *Developing Consensus, Creating Capacity, and Building Strength*. In his keynote comments, Joe Elton hailed the concept of expanding volunteer opportunities, promoted creating an umbrella organization that would provide support to individual park friends groups, and pledged his support for the group's efforts. Forty-five people attended the first conference, and by the time it ended, all were even more committed to working collaboratively to secure a successful future for all of Virginia's parks. Vera had successfully shared her vision and equipped a statewide network with the essential tools to make her vision a reality.

Developing the Plan

During the conference, the group established the following goals for the Association:

1. Foster better partnership with parks;
2. Define the "Friends" organizations in a broader context, roles, and responsibilities and bring other associated groups into that context;
3. Combine and condense Friends/Parks effort;
4. Review how decisions are being made;
5. Promote better understanding of "Friends" groups by parks;
6. Foster communication between partners; and
7. Park "selling" (persuasion).

During the conference, attendees established a Core Steering Committee of park volunteers and Friends leaders including:

- Liz Belcher, Roanoke Valley Greenway Coordinator
- J. P. Dickens, Petersburg National Park
- Susan James, Shenandoah National Park
- Robert Williams, Fredericksburg and Spotsylvania National Military Park
- Jane Yerkes, Colonial National Park

Nominees from Virginia State Parks support organizations were to be recruited.

The following park staff agreed to serve as the Park Leaders of the Core Steering Committee:

- Alec Gould, Colonial National Park
- Brian Dendis, Fredericksburg and Spotsylvania National Military Park
- Gloristine Evins, Virginia State Parks

Vera Guise of American Grassroots and Sarah Bishop of Partners in Parks were the Core Steering Committee Coaches and led the effort to establish the organization.

Conference attendees also prepared the following list of "Next Immediate Tasks" for the Steering Committee:

- Compile and distribute conference outputs
- Broaden Core Steering Committee membership to ensure equal representation of state and national parks
- Poll committee members and establish a meeting schedule for the first year
- Evaluate conference and draft recommendations for next meeting themes and goals
- Divide tasks and set timelines
- Communicate, cooperate, and coordinate!

Getting Started

When the statewide conference ended, it was time for the real work of creating an organization to fulfill the shared vision. For the next year, the Core Steering Committee met with the park leaders and coaches several times at locations across the state to build the framework for the organization. During this period, Vera Guise and Julia Hampton of American Grassroots and Sarah Bishop of Partners in Parks provided guidance and leadership. In order to create a power-sharing organization, the Core Steering Committee came from both state and national parks:

- State Parks Co-Chair: Chuck Traub, False Cape State Park
- National Parks Co-Chair: Robert Williams, Fredericksburg and Spotsylvania National Military Park
- State Parks Vice Chair: Laud Pitt, Leesylvania State Park
- National Parks Vice Chair: Susan James, Shenandoah National Park
- Treasurer: Davinder Khanna, National Park Trust

Although the titles of the officers listed above include the words "State Parks" and "National Parks," this was only an effort to ensure fair representation within the leadership. It was never the intention to limit officers, or any other members, from assisting other parks. In fact, the very purpose of this organization was to work for parks regardless of jurisdictional responsibility. The Core Steering Committee and other members frequently worked on behalf of other parks that were in close proximity to them. For example, Chuck Traub and Laud Pitt actively assisted state and national parks and their Friends groups. Robert Williams conducted a workshop to teach Virginia State Park Visitor Services Supervisors how to form Friends groups, founded a state park Friends group, and frequently wrote editorials and spoke at public meetings regarding the plight of Virginia's State Parks. This philosophy still exists within the organization. Members, especially the leadership, assist parks wherever help is needed.

Once the basic structure was in place and the Core Steering Committee was operating, Vera Guise and Sara Bishop, who had been our guides through the first year, stepped aside to pursue other professional opportunities. They had created a capable team of park leaders from all across the state, and they had prepared the team to move forward on the mission.

The Next Big Event

Now on their own, the Core Steering Committee decided to host another statewide event to continue the momentum created at the Fredericksburg conference in November 1997. In keeping with the goal of strengthening volunteer support organizations and helping to establish new support organizations, the committee decided to plan a major training event.

Robert Williams led the effort to coordinate the second statewide conference June 5-6, 1999. The host park was Prince William Forest Park, a national park in Northern Virginia. The Virginia Association for Parks, in conjunction with the Virginia Society of Certified Public Accountants (VSCPA), offered a training seminar entitled *"Managing Your Fiscal Responsibilities as a Nonprofit"* at the Ramada Inn at Quantico, Virginia, on Saturday, June 5. The purpose of the conference was to train state and national park support organizations and park staff in the basics of financial management for nonprofit organizations. Topics included discussions of how to file for nonprofit status, financial record keeping, and reporting requirements. There was ample time for questions, so the trainers could address specific needs of the park support organizations. After the training, attendees received a personal tour of Prince William Forest Park led by Park Superintendent Bob Hickman. The guest speaker for the banquet was John D. Mitchell, Director of Conservation Organizations, Virginia Department of Conservation and Recreation.

The agenda for Sunday, June 6, included a business meeting to discuss the Virginia Association for Parks' mission, bylaws, projects, future training, and to elect officers for the July 1, 1999, to June 30, 2000, term. The officers elected in November 1997 were re-elected in June 1999.

Paradigm Shift

Initially, support for the Association came primarily from the National Park Service and national organizations supporting national parks. Speaker fees and other organizational and logistical expenses for the November 1997 conference were funded by the National Park Service Northeast Region, the National Parks Conservation Association, the National Park Trust, the National Parks Mid-Atlantic Council, and Friends of Fredericksburg Area Battlefields (a National Park Friends group). The second statewide conference was also hosted by a national park.

Joe Elton, Director of Virginia State Parks, quickly saw the potential of the Virginia Association for Parks and strongly encouraged state park managers to attend the conferences and to bring a Friends group leader with them. Joe's unwavering encouragement and support for VAFP was a primary factor in the organization's early success.

At the same time Virginia's state parks were taking a more active role in VAFP, Virginia's national parks were beginning to take a less active role for the following reasons. First, the national parks in Virginia are spread among three National Park Service Regions: the Northeast Region, the National Capitol Region, and the Southeast Region. Because of this organizational structure, VAFP leadership had to coordinate with three Regional Directors located in Philadelphia, Washington, D.C., and Atlanta. Each of these Regional Directors also had multiple parks in multiple states.

Therefore, although VAFP can, and does, assist with individual national parks in Virginia, the VAFP leadership had difficulty trying to coordinate any statewide efforts on behalf of Virginia's national parks.

A second reason for the paradigm shift toward state parks is the legislative structure. With members all across the Commonwealth of Virginia, VAFP could quickly spread the word about potential threats to Virginia State Parks and have letters to the entire state legislature and letters to the editor in newspapers all across the state. On a national scale, VAFP members could contact elected officials all across Virginia, but that is still a relatively small percentage of the votes in Congress, making it difficult for VAFP to have a significant national legislative impact.

Building on the Foundation and National Attention

In 2000, the VAFP leadership team and Association members continued to build on the solid foundation that had been established in the first two years. In the spring, VAFP garnered national attention when the Association was featured in the *Saving the Legacy of the National System of Parks* report published by the National Park Trust. This article hit the newswires and was reported by environmental news organizations all across the country. The article discussed the Association's power-sharing structure and goals. *Leading the Way: Virginia Association for Parks* discussed the fact that VAFP was the first organization of its kind anywhere in the country, and that other states were interested in following the model established.

The November 2000 VAFP meeting, held at Fairy Stone State Park, proved to be a significant milestone as the Association approved several major growth steps including the unanimous approval of the Association bylaws. Chuck Traub, Co-Chair for State Parks, opened the meeting with a progress report on one of VAFP's original goals. Chuck reported that at the November 1997 conference, the Association established the goal to help start park support organizations where none existed. At that time there were nine state park support organizations. By November 2000, there were 23. Chuck noted that VAFP was at least partially responsible for this explosive growth by providing training and mentoring for old, new, and potential park support groups across the state.

Joe Elton shared two announcements. First, he shared that with a State Park budget of $19 million, Virginia now officially ranked 50th among the 50 states in terms of per capita spending on state parks. He also mentioned that although Virginia has the "most frugally managed park system" in the country, Virginia State Parks had been named a national gold medal finalist for Excellence in Park Management at the 1999 National Recreation and Park Association Annual Congress.

Robert Williams, Co-Chair for National Parks, moderated the meeting. The first order of business was to discuss and approve the Association bylaws that Robert had drafted and presented for discussion at the spring meeting at Pocahontas State Park. Robert had made the revisions suggested in the spring, so after some discussion and a few more changes, the bylaws were approved with the mission statement:

"To develop and strengthen park support organizations in Virginia."

Kayaking at Pocahontas State Park

Bylaws

The Bylaws listed the Purposes of the Association as:

A. Through participation, promote public awareness, understanding, and support for parks, forests, historic sites, and public lands in general, in cooperation with local, state, and federal agencies, as well as national, local, and regional organizations;

B. To develop excellence in citizen leadership through the sponsoring of training, technical assistance, and recognition;

C. To establish and maintain a clearinghouse of useful information, resources, and assistance for those who are committed to the responsible stewardship of public lands;

D. To develop, manage, and, when appropriate, distribute to members a statewide database of grassroots leaders, organizations, and human resource expertise to facilitate development, dialogue, and cooperation.

Other Purposes of the Association are listed as:

A. To raise funds through grants, gifts, contributions, and other mechanisms available to nonprofit organizations under the law and as deemed necessary to carry on the Association's programs and operations toward the accomplishment of its mission;

B. The Association is dedicated to and operated exclusively for not-for-profit purposes; no part of the income or assets of the Association shall be distributed to, nor to the benefit of, any individual, except through reasonable reimbursement for services rendered and expenses incurred in the course of normal operations.

Other major actions approved by the Association at the November 2000 meeting were:

A. VAFP officially adopted Virginia Park Friends as the legislative arm of VAFP;

B. VAFP established Park Mentoring Teams to serve as advisors to assist small or newly formed park support organizations. The goal was to have a Mentoring Team in every State Park district; and,

C. VAFP established Park Advocacy Teams to serve as advocates for park issues at state and national parks. The goal was to have an Advocacy Team in each State Park district to prepare editorials, letters to the editor, and have people who can speak at public meetings regarding specific park issues and concerns.

The attendees elected the following officers to two-year terms:
Co-Chair for State Parks: Laud Pitt
Co-Chair for National Parks: Robert Williams
Co-Vice Chair for State Parks: Nancy Fitzgerald
Co-Vice Chair for National Parks: Wendy Lee Oliver
Secretary: Barbara Baker
Treasurer: Davinder Khanna
Member At Large: Ann Lipp

Grayson Highlands State Park

State Incorporation

On September 25, 2001, the Virginia Association for Parks was officially incorporated by the Commonwealth of Virginia. Laud Pitt, State Parks Co-Chair, and Robert Williams, National Parks Co-Chair, signed the incorporation papers, which listed the Purposes and Powers of VAFP as:

a. To advocate for the preservation, protection, and interpretation of the natural and historic resources contained in Virginia's system of parks, including local, regional, state, and national parks located in the Commonwealth of Virginia.

b. To provide educational programs regarding these resources and how best to protect them. Educational programs will include, but not be limited to, seminars or workshops to train or assist park friends groups, park personnel, other park support organizations, and other conservation organizations.

c. To conduct service projects for Virginia's system of parks, and to assist other park support organizations with similar goals and objectives.

d. To promote for the benefit of the general public the preservation, protection, and interpretation of the natural and historic resources in the Commonwealth of Virginia.

e. To increase community appreciation, understanding, and use of the natural and historic resources through advocacy, education, protection, and preservation of land in a manner best suited for the sites, for the education, enjoyment, and benefit of present and future generations.

f. To conduct, sponsor, or facilitate special tours, lectures, conferences, seminars, and other educational activities relating to the purposes listed above.

g. To apply for and administer grants and other donations relating to the purposes of the Association and to use all assets controlled by the Association and all income thereof for the benefit of the general public and for charitable, educational, recreational, conservation, scientific, and historic purposes.

h. To aid, support, and assist by gifts, contributions, or otherwise, other corporations, community chests, funds, organizations, and foundations organized and operated exclusively for charitable, educational, or scientific purposes, no part of the earnings of which inures to the benefit of any individual, and no substantial part of the activities of which is carrying on propaganda or otherwise attempting to influence legislation.

i. To serve as an umbrella corporation for other organizations with similar goals and purposes. The Association may, as necessary, establish subsidiaries or adopt affiliates to accomplish the purposes set forth in these articles of incorporation. At no time will the Association establish or adopt a subsidiary or affiliate that does not conform to the purposes set forth in these articles. At no time will the Association establish or adopt a subsidiary or affiliate whose purposes may jeopardize the Association's non-profit tax status as listed in Article 2 of these articles of incorporation. The Association will immediately divest itself of any subsidiary or affiliate that adopts policies or procedures inconsistent with these Articles of Incorporation.

Birding at Caledon State Park- home to the Great Bald Eagle

Gold Medal Award for Excellence in Park Management

On October 3, 2001, the National Sporting Goods Association's Sports Foundation, which represents more than 22,000 retailers and 3,000 suppliers across America, presented Virginia State Parks Director Joe Elton with the coveted Gold Medal Award for Excellence in Park Management. The gold medal is given in odd-numbered years to the state park system considered most outstanding in recreational management and which best provided park, recreation, and leisure services to its citizens. Virginia's park system finished a close second in 1999 and was only the third system to garner the elite award. Ohio won in 1997, and Florida won the honor in 1999.

The award was presented at the National Recreation and Park Association's annual convention in Denver, Colorado. When receiving the award, Joe Elton stated he was particularly grateful to the hundreds of Virginia Department of Conservation and Recreation employees and thousands of volunteers who had *"dedicated tens of thousands of hours of hard work over 65 years to make Virginia's State Parks the best in the nation."*

The Virginia Association for Parks was thrilled to be able to celebrate this great honor for Virginia State Parks. Just days after winning, Joe Elton brought the award to the VAFP conference at George Washington Birthplace and stated that the Virginia Association for Parks played a prominent role in making the accomplishment possible. Joe stated that the award was, at least in part, the result of the Association's work to help establish and strengthen Virginia's state park friends groups and encourage volunteerism in state parks.

Virginia State Parks Director Joe Elton, center, holds the coveted Sports Foundation Inc. Gold Medal Award for Excellence in Park Management. He is flanked by National Park Service Director Fran Mainella and Richard Zavala, director of the Fort Worth Parks and Community Services Department, who chaired the judging panel. The award was given at the National Recreation and Park Association's annual convention on October 3, 2001, in Denver, Colorado

The Gold Medal Award for Excellence in Park Management at the podium as Robert Williams, Co-Chair for National Parks, moderates the Virginia Association For Parks meeting at George Washington Birthplace in October 2001

First Major Challenge

In the winter of 2001, the Virginia Association for Parks took on its first major challenge. Although Virginia had won the national Gold Medal Award for Excellence in Park Management in October, the dismal truth remained that Virginia ranked 50th among the 50 states in terms of per capita appropriations for state parks and proportion of state budget dedicated to state parks. This was at a time when the state was trying to cope with an ever-growing backlog of deferred maintenance and new construction needs. With the recent Gold Medal Award, the VAFP leadership believed now was the time to make a bold move to improve the situation in Virginia's state parks.   The VAFP took an active role in encouraging legislation to have a parks and recreation bond on the November 2002 ballot. The leadership was confident the people of Virginia would be willing to vote in favor of a bond for needed park repairs and improvements including:

Trail Improvements and Shoreline Erosion	$6,500,000
State Park/Natural Area Preserve Land Acquisition	$36,500,000
State Park Construction, Improvements, and Repairs	$76,040,000
Total	**$119,040,000**

The proposed project list included at least one improvement project for all 35 of Virginia's State Parks and included land acquisition funding for six new state parks and 10 new Natural Area Preserves. The Natural Area Preserve System includes examples of some of the rarest natural communities and rare species habitats in Virginia.   Although some Natural Area Preserves are open to the public, they are not managed by the Virginia State Park System.

**Inside new cabins at
Natural Tunnel built from
2002 General Obligation Bond**

Thirty-one of Virginia's 35 parks were on the proposed list to receive significant new construction, improvements, or repairs to facilities. These included cabins, campgrounds, docks, piers, picnic shelters, park roads, utilities, offices, visitor centers, and repairs to historic structures.

During the legislative session, VAFP members contacted their state legislators to express their support for this bond and to explain why these funds were so desperately needed. Other major conservation organizations also supported the referendum, and the State Legislature approved the measure.

Obtaining legislation for the bond referendum was only the first step. VAFP now had to convince a majority of the voters that these funds were a worthwhile investment of taxpayer dollars. Members of the VAFP participated in strategic planning meetings with Department of Conservation and Recreation officials. Members from all across the state wrote letters to the editor of their area newspapers and spoke with friends and at public meetings, to explain the purpose of the referendum and to encourage support for our state parks.

**Accessible pier at
Belle Isle State Park**

Governor Mark Warner invited the Virginia Association for Parks to join him at a bond referendum media event at Shenandoah River State Park on June 6. VAFP Co-Chairs Laud Pitt and Robert Williams were asked to stand with Governor Warner as he addressed the media to discuss the need for the bond referendum, and VAFP members Jo and Johnny Finch were interviewed on the Governor's video media release and several radio programs.

On November 8, when all the votes were counted, Virginians overwhelmingly voted in favor of the Parks and Recreational Facilities Bond, allowing the $119 million bond referendum to pass with more than 69% of the vote. The Virginia Association for Parks had accomplished its first major challenge in support of Virginia's State Parks.

State Parks Co-Chair Laud Pitt presents Governor Warner with an Honorary Membership in the Virginia Association For Parks. From left to right: Laud Pitt, Governor Warner, Robert Williams, DCR Director Joe Maroon, Delegate Clay Athey, Joe Elton, Virginia State Parks Director, and Governor Warner's Press Secretary, Kevin Hall

Cabin at James River State Park funded by the 2002 GOB for which Virginians overwhelmingly voted to support improvements to their state parks

Reaching Out

The Virginia Association for Parks 2002 fall conference was held at Hungry Mother State Park in Marion, Virginia, and represented the five-year anniversary of the organization. This meeting was also a first for the group because it was the first time the organization had reached beyond state and national parks. At this meeting, the VAFP leadership also invited Friends groups from Virginia's national forests and national wildlife refuges, which are part of the US Fish and Wildlife Service. On Friday, September 6, the meeting agenda included a tour of Mt. Rogers National Recreation Area in the Jefferson National Forest and a tour of Grayson Highlands State Park. The Friday agenda also included a presentation of the status of Virginia's national forests and a wild land fire management policy presentation from the US Forest Service. During lunch, Sandy Rives, Virginia Parks Coordinator for the National Park Service, and Joe Elton, Director of Virginia State Parks, conducted a joint presentation regarding how the VAFP model was helping to create a seamless system of parks in Virginia. The Friday evening banquet speaker was Dave Muhly, Associate Regional Representative of the Sierra Club Appalachian Region. His topic was clean air initiatives.

The Saturday agenda included a presentation from the US Fish and Wildlife Service discussing the status of wildlife unique to the southwest Virginia area. Lynn Davis, Director of Public Affairs at the Virginia Tech College of Natural Resources, conducted a training presentation on "Advocating For Your Park (PR 101)." Lynn Davis was a founding member of the Friends of the Blue Ridge Parkway and an advisor to Vera Guise when Vera was forming the Virginia Association for Parks.

A fun-filled summer day at Lake Anna State Park

During the business portion of the meeting, the VAFP membership approved the organization's first by-laws change. The revision instituted staggered terms of office for VAFP board members. This issue became a concern over the summer when the board realized that VAFP would be losing two of its original board members at this election. Neither Laud Pitt, Co-Chair for State Parks, nor Robert Williams, Co-Chair for National Parks, were seeking re-election in the fall. Without staggered terms, there was a concern that at some point, the organization could lose all of its leadership at one time. The by-laws change was approved, and a new slate of officers was elected for the following terms:

Co-Chair (State Parks): Johnny Finch (one year)
Co-Chair (National Parks): Wendy Lee Oliver (two years)
Vice Chair (State Parks): Nancy Fitzgerald (two years)
Vice Chair (National Parks): Lynn Davis (one year)
Treasurer: Davinder Khanna (two years)
Secretary: Barbara Baker (one year)
Member-at-Large: Ann Lipp (two years)

Following the 2002 Fall Conference, VAFP management completed and filed the requisite annual VAFP report to the State Corporation Commission and the requisite annual registration package with the State Office of Consumer Affairs. They also sought legal assistance in filling out a 501(c)(3) application to file with the Internal Revenue Service to seek approval for VAFP to have tax exempt nonprofit status.

The response from the legal community indicated a willingness to do the needed work in return for significant legal fees – fees that far exceeded VAFP's small bank balance at the time. Given that a major part of VAFP's mission is to help Friends groups form and file the requisite paperwork, management decided to wade through the process themselves as a learning experience that could be used in helping Friends groups get through the same process.

The resulting application to the IRS was successful, and VAFP was officially approved as a tax exempt nonprofit organization on November 13, 2002. After receiving IRS approval, VAFP terminated its fiduciary relationship with the National Park Trust and established its own bank account.

Receipt of 501(c)(3) status was a seminal event in VAFP's history. Without that designation, many of VAFP's subsequent successes would not have been possible.

Park users hike and bike the historic High Bridge Trail State Park

The Growth Years (2002-2011)

The year 2002 was an important transitional year in VAFP's history in that the organization began to become more publicly active on several fronts. It was during this year that the organization began to move exponentially from the 1997 vision toward the reality of the significant and respected position it holds today within Virginia's natural resources community.

Pivotal steps along the way included recognizing and acting on the need to set goals and change the organizational structure to better ensure success; developing and implementing an advocacy process that built on the success achieved with the 2002 bond referendum; and, anticipating the economic downturn that came to be, realizing that appropriated funds would need to be supplemented with grant and donation dollars, and successfully adapting to that need. But throughout VAFP's 15-year history, the most important ingredient for its organizational success has been the strong support provided by the ever devout, energetic, responsive, and growing membership.

Strategic Goals—The Guiding Beacons

A great part of VAFP's success can be attributed to the organization's recognition of the need to set strategic goals for management's guidance and the willingness to change organizational structure as needed to better achieve those goals. At the 2003 Spring Conference, VAFP adopted strategic long-range goals and an action plan. The goals included:

- creating a more seamless organization;
- enhancing VAFP's legislative presence;
- increasing VAFP's operating revenue; and
- expanding VAFP's structure and the resulting membership base.

These goals have been remarkably resilient and continue today to guide and focus management's attention. They thus provide an excellent framework for chronicling major portions of VAFP's history.

Fishing at Claytor Lake State Park

Creating a More Seamless Organization

The strategic goals resulted in management considering whether VAFP had the right organizational structure for achieving them. The organizational structure at the time of the 2003 Spring Conference when the goals were adopted consisted of a seven person slate of officers: Co-Chair (State Parks), Co-Chair (National Parks), Vice-Chair (State Parks), Vice-Chair (National Parks), Treasurer, Secretary, and Member-at-Large.

Given the ill health of the Co-Chair (National Parks) and the overfull personal schedule of the Vice-Chair (National Parks), the Co-Chair (State Parks) agreed in late 2002 to temporarily take on responsibilities for both state park and national park issues. Based largely on the ensuing experience, management began to actively pursue the strategic goal of creating a more seamless organization to help enhance public perception. The initial "twin smoke-stack" organizational structure was clearly effective in terms of forming and launching VAFP. Given VAFP's increasing public activity, it now seemed that there were benefits to be gained by assuring the public that VAFP was truly a united effort to support Virginia's parks versus a "two separate camps" entity.

Thus, the Nominating Committee recommended to the attendees at the 2003 Fall Conference that the by-laws be amended to create the position of President and to eliminate the position of Member-at-Large. While the number of elected officers would remain at seven, the President's duties would be to serve as the official spokesperson for the Association and to provide strategic and operational direction to the Association's long-range goals and daily activities.

The proposed amendment passed by unanimous vote and the Nominating Committee proposed a new slate of officers for the ensuing election. In compiling the new slate, the Committee took into consideration that, Barbara Baker had resigned from the Secretary position earlier in the year, and, at the 2003 Spring Conference, Jo Finch had volunteered to complete Barbara's term; and, secondly that Davinder Khana also wanted to step down as Treasurer.

The new slate of officers proposed by the Nominating Committee at the 2003 Fall Conference were: Johnny Finch, President; Wendy Lee Oliver, Co-Chair (National Parks); Nancy Fitzgerald, Co-Chair (State Parks); Lynn Davis, Vice Co-Chair (National Parks); John Taminger, Vice Co-Chair (State Parks); Ann Lipp, Treasurer; and Jo Finch, Secretary. The recommended slate of officers was unanimously approved by the attendees.

As VAFP completed its activities in 2003 and moved into 2004, management continued to gain experience with implementing the strategic goals adopted in 2003 and came to believe that further benefits in terms of enhanced organizational efficiency, effectiveness, and public perception could be derived from making VAFP's organization even more seamless. To this end, management decided to propose to the membership a further streamlining of the elected officer positions.

At the 2004 Fall Conference, the Nominating Committee recommended to the attendees that the two Vice Chair positions be eliminated, and that the duties of the Co-Chair and President positions be redefined accordingly. The Nominating Committee also presented to the attendees proposed amendments to the by-laws to accomplish these recommendations and a recommended slate of officers to fill the streamlined positions. The recommendations, including the proposed slate of officers and the proposed by-law amendments, passed unanimously.

The number of elected officers was thus reduced from seven to five; the five elected were Johnny Finch, President; Wendy Lee Oliver, National Parks Chair; Nancy Fitzgerald, State Parks Chair; Ann Lipp, Treasurer; and Jo Finch, Secretary. Wendy Lee Oliver subsequently announced her resignation and Lynn Davis agreed to complete Wendy's term.

The foregoing officers, including Lynn Davis, were re-elected each time the respective terms were completed until 2006. In 2006, Nancy Fitzgerald stepped down from her position as Chair of State Parks. The Nominating Committee recommended James Klakowicz to be Nancy's replacement, and he was duly elected. The slate of officers has remained constant since that time, being duly re-elected when respective terms expired.

Enhancing VAFP's Legislative Presence

The 2002 $119 million bond referendum was VAFP's first significant visible foray into the public sector. Flushed with the success of that effort, VAFP's management and membership was eager to do more in support of Virginia's parks. A clear opportunity for doing so was available and quickly acted on.

Chippokes Plantation State Park, located on the James River, features a variety of historic tours and programming, plus fantastic natural adventure along the river

In an earlier legislative session, the General Assembly had created a bi-cameral, bi-partisan commission–"The Commission on the Future of Virginia's Environment." The Commission's charge was to investigate related issues and provide the Assembly with a report including recommendations for needed actions. The Co-Chairs of the Commission's Natural Resources Subcommittee were Delegate (at the time, now Senator) Creigh Deeds and Senator Emmett Hanger.

The Commission's report and recommendations were issued in 2002 in Senate Document 4. The Commission noted that a 1992 publicly approved state parks bond referendum had provided $95 million for acquisition of land and construction of new facilities, that the bond money could be used for the stipulated purposes only, and that operating and maintenance money for the newly constructed facilities was to be provided through increased annual budget appropriations, but that the annual appropriations had not kept pace with the operational and maintenance funding need as new facilities were completed and brought on line.

To cover the deficiency in needed funding for new facilities that were already on line, the Commission recommended that the state park system's operating and maintenance budget be re-benchmarked to provide $12.2 million in the first year of funding and $8.3 million for each subsequent year. VAFP quickly adopted the Committee's recommendations and began developing a strategy to help ensure that the recommendations were implemented by the General Assembly.

Implementation of that strategy began in late 2002 with VAFP letters to the Governor, the Secretary of Natural Resources, the Chairs and members of the House Appropriations Committee, the Senate Finance Committee, and the relevant Subcommittees.

In early 2003, VAFP continued its letter-writing effort and supplemented that effort with a physical presence in Richmond during the General Assembly session. VAFP members talked to as many Delegates, Senators, and staff as possible and left each with point sheets to help jog their memories about the state park system's financial and personnel needs. VAFP members also testified before pertinent House and Senate Subcommittees during the course of the legislative session.

VAFP has continued its mantra over the years using this same basic approach. In recent years the approach was supplemented by designing and wearing shirts prominently displaying the VAFP logo when attending Assembly sessions and in meetings with individual legislators and staff members. The shirts have now become readily recognized by key legislators and staff in the General Assembly building. Also, for the past few years, VAFP has partnered with the Virginia Broadcasters Association to host receptions during key committee and subcommittee retreats. This has provided outstanding access and education opportunities.

VAFP 2009 Spring Conference at Westmoreland State Park

Jim Klakowicz, State Parks Chair; Clyde Cristman, Senate Finance Committee Staff; Ann Lipp, Treasurer; Johnny Finch, President; Joe Elton, VSP Director; Delegate Albert Pollard; Lynn Davis, National Parks Chair; Jo Finch, Secretary

As time passed, VAFP recognized that the same situation noted by the Commission for the 1992 bond constructed facilities was happening for the facilities being constructed and brought on line from the 2002 bond referendum proceeds – annual appropriations were not meeting the operations and maintenance need. Thus, VAFP worked with the Department of Conservation and Recreation to determine the appropriation shortfall and used that number to adjust the total re-benchmarking need. VAFP also created a "Re-benchmarking Status" document, updated it yearly, and included it along with the annual point sheet given to key legislators and staff.

To better ensure that members knew when and how to contact key legislators, the VAFP leadership team focused on recording accurate membership contact information, relying heavily on email addresses. Next, the team adopted a "communications tree" approach for notifying the membership of events taking place, the need for action on the membership's part, the persons who should be contacted, and the pertinent contact information needed to reach those persons. Each member was asked to forward the information to family, friends, neighbors, co-workers, and other interested persons.

Virginians love their parks! The VAFP membership has been extremely supportive and fiercely responsive in reacting to management's "calls to action." The VAFP President takes great pride in illustrating the membership's responsiveness by relating the following event whenever the opportunity arises.

The President had been on extended travel, had returned home late on a Friday, and had started "digging out from under" the correspondence back-log. In doing so, he learned that the National Parks Conservation Association (NPCA) was seeking help in getting the U.S. Congress' attention better focused on the visual pollution problems facing the national parks.

To this end, NPCA had devised a national contest centered on e-post cards. The idea was for individuals to send an e-post card to their Congressional delegation calling attention to the visual pollution problem and then to encourage as many other people as possible to do the same. NPCA had a way to track the results and determine who succeeded in generating the most postcards.

Clearly, this effort fell within VAFP's mission. Even though the contest had already been underway for several weeks and this was the Saturday before the contest was to end on Monday, the VAFP President endorsed the NPCA effort, sent the requisite e-post card to Virginia's Congressional delegation, and then sent a message to the VAFP membership briefly explaining the issue and asking them to participate.

The following Tuesday, the VAFP President received a congratulatory telephone call from NPCA thanking him for having generated the most e-post cards in the national contest. The second and third place winners were from California and New York, both states having larger populations than Virginia. This result speaks volumes about the outstanding dedication, support, and responsiveness of the VAFP membership.

Appropriation Impacts

During the 2002-2011 timeframe, Virginia's state park system consistently ranked among (when not solely in last place) the most frugally funded state park systems across the nation in terms of per capita appropriations. Given this context, VAFP takes great pride in having been instrumental in obtaining legislative budget amendments that achieved appropriation increases totaling $12.5 million and 108 new authorized positions for the state park system over the 2003-2008 time frame. Over the 2009-2011 time frame, VAFP helped restore 15 positions and $2.7 million of $5 million in budget cuts imposed in response to the deteriorating economy.

Increasing VAFP's Operating Revenue

In 2002, VAFP's bank balance was considerably less than $500. Being an all volunteer organization with no paid staff and no infrastructure overhead in terms of office space and equipment, the organization was able to move forward using the revenue from membership dues, conference registrations, and small donations.

During 2006 and into 2007, VAFP management anticipated a downturn in the economy, realized that future appropriations for the park system would not be in keeping with those of the past few years, and began seeking opportunities to supplement future appropriations with cash from grants and increased private sector donations. This strategy proved fruitful as shown by the following examples.

Automated Information Stations

During a meeting with VAFP management, the State Parks Director mentioned that he had recently attended an out-of-state conference where new technology was displayed to demonstrate the possibility of having interactive, user-friendly, automated information readily available to park visitors. The Director was excited about the possibilities presented, his excitement was contagious, and his vision proved profound.

This led to an informal partnership between the state park system, VAFP, and Imperial Multimedia - the Wisconsin based company owned by Fred Lochner- that had demonstrated the technology. Working together, a grant proposal was developed and VAFP, being the nonprofit member of the partnership, submitted the proposal to the Dominion Foundation. Dominion responded by funding the proposal to the tune of $300,000.

With this funding, 32 automated information stations were installed across the park system. Subsequently, Dominion funded a VAFP proposal for $50,000 to complete the project so that an information station became available in each of the system's 35 parks.

The automated information stations allowed users to obtain detailed information, including printing out trail maps for the host park as well as for the other 34 parks in the system. Thus, if a user was planning a trip through Virginia that centered on visits to multiple state parks, the user could preplan the trip from any of the park information stations. A 2010 study performed by Virginia Tech showed that the number of park visitors who used the information stations had increased significantly over the previous year and that the users reported a higher overall satisfaction rating for their park visit than did non-users.

Once the information stations were up and running, VAFP, the park system, and Imperial Multimedia collaborated to develop a new grant proposal to seek funding for taking all of the information available from the automated stations and supplementing that information to provide a much richer content that would then be made available on the internet.

To establish the website, VAFP submitted a proposal to Dominion which responded with funding of $350,000. This funding was used to create a website at www.virginiaoutdoors.com where anyone with a computer from anywhere in the world could not only access detailed information about any and all of Virginia's state parks, including the ability to take a virtual tour of the subject park as well as view and print out trail maps, but could also access detailed information on numerous outdoor recreational opportunities across the Commonwealth. Content is added to this website virtually on a daily basis, and the site has become the premier source for outdoor recreation information across the state. The funding also enabled Imperial Multimedia to update VAFP's business website located at www.virginiaparks.org. The updating provides VAFP with the ability to communicate with its membership on matters of immediate interest as well as to list the state park projects that VAFP is seeking to fund and to enable donors to make dues payments and donations to specific projects through PayPal.

VAFP seized the opportunity through the new websites to fully address another strategic goal adopted in 2003. It was aimed at expanding the membership by increasing the membership

categories available to those wishing to join VAFP. In the organization's early history, membership categories were individual and organizational.

The categories now range from "Associate Member" to "Platinum Member," with the Associate level being free and the other levels ranging in dollar amounts to the Platinum level of $1,000 and up annually. Membership benefits vary with each level. From the handful of individuals who came together in 1997, VAFP's membership currently numbers in the thousands. VAFP leadership hopes that as the membership numbers continue to increase, VAFP will be able to derive a revenue stream from the www.virginiaoutdoors.com site by providing outdoor recreation industries and retail suppliers with a direct link on the site for a "to be determined" fee. This revenue, as is the case with all VAFP generated revenues, will be devoted in its entirety to the state park system.

Smartphone App

Another technology initiative, a smartphone app, allows the content from the information stations, the websites, and other sources to be accessed through smartphones, thus providing the ultimate in data portability. Virginia State Parks are now as close as your smartphone through the use of the Virginia State Parks Pocket Ranger application. This app was made possible through a couple of public-private partnerships.

Developed collaboratively through the Virginia Department of Conservation and Recreation and ParksByNature, the new app is made available at no charge through a partnership between Imperial Multimedia and VAFP. Imperial and VAFP are also nearing completion of a sponsorship plan so that app users will be supporting Virginia State Parks each time the app is used.

The foregoing examples and other VAFP efforts to increase operating revenue have been remarkably successful, especially given the deteriorating economy. In the 2007-2011 time frame, VAFP generated more than $1 million in cash grants and donations for investment in the park system.

Awards and Recognition Given

Over the years, VAFP has developed and given two basic awards, one for legislators and one for non-legislators.

Legislator of the Year Award

As mentioned earlier, Virginia has had the unwanted distinction of ranking among (when not solely in position of last place) the most frugally funded state park systems across the nation in terms of per capita appropriations.

To recognize long-term, dedicated legislative support for the park system, VAFP created a Legislator of the Year Award, and has consistently held the position that this award must truly be earned over time and is not to become viewed as an expected annual event.

Over an eight-year time frame, five such awards have been bestowed, the first being given in 2003 to Delegate Jim Dillard, now retired. Subsequent awards have been given to Senator Creigh Deeds, Senator Emmett Hanger, Delegate Watkins Abbitt, and Senator Mary Margaret Whipple.

Management recognized that non-legislators also help to further VAFP's success and gave thought to a suitable award to bestow in this regard. The resulting award was named in honor of a favorite phrase of Joe Elton, State Parks Director. In discussing the actions of an individual, group, or organization, Joe is fond of saying..."They are my heroes."

Fittingly, the first "Our Hero" Award was bestowed on Joe Elton in recognition of his stellar long-term leadership of the state park system, his support of VAFP, and his election as President of the National Association of State Park Directors. Subsequent awards were bestowed on:

• Nancy Heltman, Park System Visitor Services Manager, for her efforts to lead the park system and VAFP into the world of social networking;

• Friends of Lake Anna State Park for accomplishing the major feat of funding the purchase and installation of a $30,000 toddler playground train;

• Clyde Cristman, Senate Finance Committee staff, for invaluable help in budget analysis; and,

• Sharon B. Ewing, Park System Chief of Cultural Resources and Park Manager of the Southwest Virginia Museum Historical State Park, for authoring a coffee table book on the history of Virginia's state parks and dedicating the financial proceeds to VAFP.

Awards and Recognition Received

Over the years, VAFP has received awards and recognition in several forms, including being recognized by having a member(s) appointed to special external committees or commissions with objectives having significant import for the Commonwealth's natural resources.

In 2003, VAFP's growing stature was acknowledged by the presence of three members attending the "by invitation only" Governor's Natural Resources Summit Conference. During this conference, Secretary of Natural Resources Tayloe Murphy asked VAFP's President to serve as a Governor appointee to a special ad hoc committee charged with a six-month effort to formulate recommendations to the Governor on how Virginia could better market its natural resources for tourism purposes. This committee was co-chaired by the Secretary of Natural Resources and the Secretary of Commerce and Trade.

Also in 2003, Joe Elton, State Parks Director, presented VAFP with a framed commendation for its efforts. It read:

"Virginia State Parks hereby commends the Virginia Association for Parks for its efforts to pass the 2002 State Parks and Natural Areas Bond Referendum and Dedicated Advocacy during the 2003 session of the Virginia General Assembly."

The document was signed by the Director of the Department of Conservation and Recreation, the Director of Virginia State Parks, by the Assistant Director of State Parks, and the Manager of each state park in Virginia.

In 2004, the VAFP President was asked to become a member of the Governor's Natural Resource Partnership Committee and, in 2006, was asked to be a member of the Governor-Elect's Natural Resource Policy Transition Committee. This committee was charged with producing a draft natural resources policy manual for the Governor-elect and the soon-to-be-appointed Secretary of Natural Resources.

In 2007, VAFP received national recognition in the form of the National Association of State Park Directors (NASPD) President's Award, inscribed:

"In recognition of your outstanding service, commitment and leadership to preserve, protect and enhance our natural and cultural state park resources in the great state of Virginia."

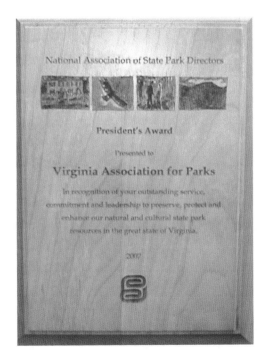

At Hungry Mother State Park, for the 75th anniversary celebration - speaking about the CCC and those who led the effort to build and launch our state park system on June 15, 1936, Governor Bob McDonnell stated: "They had the foresight and vision to create what truly now is ranked year in and year out the  greatest state park system in America, and I would note that it also has got the least amount of funding per capita in any park system, we're trying to improve that, but it shows it's more than money, it's heart and soul, and vision, it's entrepreneurship that makes a great park system." Photo at celebration, left to right: Patty Elton, Governor Bob McDonnell, and State Parks Director, Joe Elton.

Johnny Finch presents Senator Ralph Northam a history of Virginia State Parks at the 2012 Spring Conference held at Kiptopeke State Park

Dedicated VAFP members brave the weather at one of the overlooks of "the Grand Canyon of the South" at Breaks Interstate Park during the 2011 VAFP Fall Conference

VAFP Executive Committee members with Delegate Watkins Abbitt after his Legislator of the Year presentation. Left to right: Nancy Heltman, State Parks Visitor Services Manager; Jim Klakowicz, State Parks Chair; Ann Lipp, Treasurer; Delegate Abbitt; Johnny Finch, President; Jo Finch, Secretary; Lynn Davis, National Parks Chair; Joe Elton, State Parks Director

The people who work solely as individuals or join others to form groups to work in support of individual parks across the Commonwealth truly form the heart and soul of the volunteer effort. VAFP has recognized this truism since 1997 and has worked diligently each year to help such groups form and continue. Assistance provided to groups has included start-up funding; templates to use, and hands-on assistance, in completing the requisite by-laws, articles of incorporation, and 501(c)(3) application paperwork; semiannual conferences providing training and networking opportunities; and no term/no interest loans for funding selected local projects in state parks.

Friends of James River State Park at the 2009 VAFP Fall Conference

The Heart of Volunteerism: Friends Groups' Histories

The growth in volunteer support for the state park system has been nothing short of astounding. In 2000, about 40,000 volunteer hours of service were donated to the state park system. In 2011, over 6,000 volunteers donated more than 343,000 hours of service to the system. The Department of Conservation and Recreation has valued the 2011 volunteer contribution at $7.5 million and the equivalent of 165 full-time positions. Information about established Virginia State Parks "Friends Groups" follows with each park listed alphabetically.

Friends of High Bridge Trail State Park were instrumental in supporting the park's development

Friends of Holliday Lake State Park work on the site's Butterfly Garden

Volunteers at Bear Creek Lake State Park cleanup downed trees after a storm

Friends of Bear Creek Lake State Park

Organized: In Spring of 2009, interested residents from Cumberland, Buckingham and Powhatan counties first met. In 2011, the group filed for 501(c)(3) status.

Key Organizers: Initial officers were Bobby Wilcox, President; Patty Elton, Vice-President; Deborah Kennell, Secretary; and Cecil Youngblood, Treasurer. There are nearly 40 individuals from the three communities who stay up-to-date with the happenings of FBCLSP; a courageous dozen have accomplished much.

Mission: The Friends are volunteers dedicated to the development of educational and entertaining programs for all ages on topics covering the environment and responsibility of land stewardship and conservation.

Projects: Some of the Friends' projects have included:
- Hosting park's trail dedication, 70th anniversary and cabin open house; anniversary video created by Youth Ambassador;
- Providing meals for the Youth Conservation Corps;
- Participating in the Odwalla Tree Campaign, Cumberland Patriot Day, Central Piedmont Virginia Master Naturalist's Bluebird Workshop, and the park's Wildflower Symposium;
- Managing the park's Archery Range which boasts 10 lanes and 3-D targets;
- Building two new native gardens in the park;
- Assisting in cleaning the Bear Creek Hall carpets;
- Submitting a grant to the National Environmental Education Foundation;
- Preparing a meal for the graduating class of Bear Creek Academy and hosting picnic for the Central Virginia Chapter of Heroes on the Water, a wounded warrior nonprofit; and,
- Monitoring bird boxes, participating in Longwood University's Wellness Fair, attending the Cumberland County Schools Community Day and the Survival Garden Dedication, serving lunch to Cumberland County Historical Tour participants, and conducting a gently used book sale.

Friends of Belle Isle State Park

Organized: First organizational meeting in October 2000 and incorporated with the IRS in August 2001.

Key Organizers: Long before Belle Isle State Park had an official Friends group, the Park had an active friend, Lynn Larson. By the spring of 1999, she had already helped with several projects throughout the park, including restoring the Bel Air gardens, trail work, and assisting at the Summer Family Fun Fest. With a handful of friends and new acquaintances, Lynn planned the first organized "interest" meeting on October 25, 2000.

Mission: From their beginning, the Friends of Belle Isle have actively supported the park. However, one theme has emerged as their top priority: to provide affordable or free activities that can be enjoyed by families and youth.

Projects: Since its inception, the Friends of Belle Isle have contributed over 5,000 hours in volunteer time and funded programs and projects totaling over $75,000, including:

- Organize "Music by the River" free concerts each summer where the Friends give away popcorn and sell drinks at the concert, and assist park staff at the children's crafts and games area;
- Began an Easter Egg hunt, co-hosted the Youth Outdoors Day, Halloween Haunted Trail, and the Family Fall Festival;
- Provided meals to the Youth Conservation Corps members and their families and donated $1,000 to YCC in 2004;
- Helped cover the Virginia State Park booth at the State Fair of Virginia;
- Conducted bi-annual "Adopt a Highway" road trash pickup and maintain native plant gardens;
- Contributed $900 toward hosting the "Blowin' the Dust Off" tour; and,
- Received a $27,222 grant to construct a handicap accessible boardwalk and fishing pier.

Friends of Caledon State Park

Organized: First organized in 2001.

Key Organizers: Robert Williams, Margie Brewer-Zambon, John LoBuglio, Cindy Harry, and Joan Mudd. Jim Lynch, Laurie Schlemm, Darryl Breitenstien, and Rob Williams are current long term members.

Mission: The Friends of Caledon actively participate in the mission of Caledon State Park. Caledon protects and preserves the native flora and fauna, including bald eagles, as well as historical and cultural resources.

Projects: Since its inception, Friends members have contributed over 8,000 hours of volunteer time and over $15,000 to the park. Examples of funded efforts include:
- Water feature and surrounding garden that is part of the accessible trail and garden;
- Benches for the hay wagon used for program transportation;
- Materials for the renovation of several bridges and board-walks along the hiking trail system;
- Materials for children's interpretive programs and birdseed for the visitor center displays;
- Annual Art and Wine Festival;
- New live tank displays in the visitor center discovery room; funded nest box maintenance and continue to monitor a blue-bird trail in the park;
- Public address system for use in interpretive programs;
- Materials and supplies for Haunted Halloween Programs at the natural area;
- Several landscape projects within the park;
- Materials for the three Backyard Campout programs; and,
- Provided hundreds of hours of hiking trail maintenance.

Friends of Chippokes Plantation State Park

Organized: Discussion of forming the Friends group began with park staff in 1998. The group became official in January 1999.

Key Organizers: The Friends group organizers included: JoAn Miller, President; Barbara Lindley, Vice President; Dee van den Brink, Secretary; Helen and Victor Lennox, Treasurers.

Mission: A dedicated core of volunteers organized Friends of Chippokes to provide support for the park through volunteer services and fundraising.

Projects: The Friends have contributed over 20,000 volunteer hours and funded programs and projects totaling over $80,000. Accomplishments include:
- Opened a gift shop;
- Established an equestrian area with eight miles of trails;
- Conducted an annual Easter Egg Hunt;
- Funded Chippokes orientation film, *A Jewel on the James*;
- Published Chippokes historical recipe book, *Eating and Drinking Like a Virginia Planter*, and later a second edition, *Looking Back at Chippokes Plantation*;
- Funded restoration of the 1941 Packard that belonged to the last owners of the plantation;
- Purchased two golf carts for park hosts, as well as benches, porch furniture, refrigerator, microwave, TV, tables, materials for storage shed and recycling bins, and wood splitter;
- Created Friends website: *www.chippokes.com*;
- Volunteered for garden workdays, mansion docents, gift shop, archiving historical records on computer, supplying firewood, and assisting with public events and activities; and,
- Funded MP-3 players for Chippokes' first self-guided audio-visual tour of the park.

Friends of Douthat State Park

Organized: Douthat State Park called a meeting in 1997 to put together a special event known as the Douthat Lake Run Cruise In and Car Show. The car show planning began, and Douthat State Park Environmental Education (SPEED) was born.

Key Organizers: Douthat SPEED is organized exclusively for charitable, scientific, and educational purposes.   The group is working toward 501(c)(3) certification.

Mission: Douthat SPEED partners with Douthat State Park and the community to provide exciting educational opportunities fostering environmental stewardship.

Projects: SPEED projects include:
- Douthat Lake Run Cruise In and Car Show held annually. The event includes music and games on the beach with hundreds of classic autos. All registration fees and other money raised throughout the weekend are given to SPEED;
- For years, the group has been working towards making Douthat's Discovery Center a reality. The Discovery Center is planned to be at a historic building constructed by the Civilian Conservation Corps. Plans have been drawn up and include renovating the Civilian Conservation Corps structure and creating an up-to-date facility, with an audio visual great room, a wet lab for field work, restrooms, shower facilities, and offices. The room will also house displays for people who visit the center to learn the ecology of the park; and,
- Douthat Arts and Crafts Fair, held the last Saturday of each July, allows local artisans and crafters to sell and showcase their goods to the community. There is a fee ranging from $20 per booth to $65 per booth which is given to the Douthat SPEED.

Friends of Fairy Stone State Park

Organized: The Friends of Fairy Stone formed in 1986 as a way for the park to accept donations for the Junior Ranger program. The Bassett Walker Corporation, a local textile manufacturer, wanted to donate money so that the program could be offered without charge.

Key Organizers: In the early days of the Friends group, Mary and Ronnie Haynes, who run the Haynes 57 gas station at the Fairy Stone hunt site, handled the treasurer duties. They collected the donations and reimbursed the park for supplies used in the Junior Ranger program. Most of the Friends group projects are now handled by Tim Collins, the current Friends of Fairy Stone president.

Mission: To provide financial and in-kind support to Fairy Stone as it endeavors to provide recreational opportunities to park visitors and preserve park resources for future generations.

Projects: Over the years, the Friends group helped out with the first Children's Fishing program and paid for some bluegrass performances. After the first year, the Children's Fishing program was taken over by the local fishing club, and Reynolds Homestead started paying for several music shows each year. By 2004, the original group was no longer active. The current Friends group was revived and these efforts have taken place since 2005:

- Organized a classic car show;
- Partially funded an Eagle Scout project to build a fire pit and benches for interpretive programs;
- Started an annual Boy Scout spring camporee and volunteer day, which led to the completion of many trail projects;
- Conducted outreach programs at the Virginia Museum of Natural History and local schools; and,
- Assisted interpreters performing programs for large school groups visiting the park.

Friends of False Cape State Park

Organized: The Friends group was originally formed in 1989 and is currently undergoing a revitalization and reorganization effort.

Key Organizers: Diana Ramsey, Bob Safford, and Bruce Julian.

Mission: The Friends are a group of park supporters who assist the park in achieving its goals of serving visitors and protecting park resources.

False Cape State Park: a unique coastal experience on the Atlantic Ocean

Projects: Since its inception, the Friends of False Cape State Park have contributed over 10,000 volunteer hours and donated nearly $20,000. The Friends of False Cape have assisted with or are currently assisting with funding and volunteer efforts for the following projects:
- Visitor Center;
- Operations Clean the Bay Day;
- International Coastal Clean-Up;
- Hunt Operations;
- Overlook construction;
- Trail construction and maintenance; and,
- Advocacy at the city, state, and national level.

Friends of First Landing State Park

Organized: The Friends of First Landing was formed in 1987. The group's first priority was to develop by-laws and incorporate as a nonprofit organization for the purpose of accepting cash donations and materials in support of a native plant landscaping project at the park's Visitor Center.

Key Organizers: The first meeting of the Friends was on October 18, 1987. Delegate Harry R. Purkey was the guest speaker. A nominating committee chaired by Fred Shubart was formed to identify potential officers. Irma Reagan served as the first President (1988-90) and, with professional guidance from John Egan, the Friends obtained 501(c)(3) tax status in 1989. Currently, the membership boasts 87 people.

Mission: The mission is to assist the Virginia State Parks with the continued preservation and conservation of a National Natural Landmark and one of Virginia's six original state parks, Seashore.

Projects: Several Friends projects include:
- Under the leadership of Delegate Bob Purkey, joined by Delegate Glenn Croshaw and City Councilmen Billy Harrison and Will Sessoms, the Friends raised about $6,000 toward exhibits for the new Chesapeake Bay Center;
- In 2007, the Friends were heavily involved in the planning and implementation of the Jamestown 400th Anniversary First Landing Re-enactment events;
- In 2009, the Friends re-organized in an effort to capitalize on a new partnership with the Princess Anne Garden Club to fund exhibits at the newly built LEED certified Trail Center; and,
- The Friends currently assist with funding and volunteer efforts, for advocacy on behalf of the park, fundraising for volunteer events, and sponsoring the First Landing Tree Army and Fall Fest events.

Friends of Grayson Highlands State Park

Organized: The Friends of Grayson Highlands incorporated on September 1, 2004.

Key Organizers: Bill Ballinger was elected first President; Doug Niemi, Vice President; Donna Niemi, Treasurer; Gail Josey as Secretary, with Kenneth and Sue Weaver as main supporters. The Friends group has grown to 35 members.

Mission: The Friends identify and promote activities to preserve, conserve, and enhance the natural, historical, cultural, scenic, educational, and recreational resources of the park.

Projects: Friends members have contributed 12,350 volunteer hours and over $13,375 for projects that include:

- Financial assistance with junior rangers programs, dog show, October Hayride, Easter Egg Hunt, Youth Conservation Corps programs, and Odwalla Tree program;
- Provided recycling containers for aluminum and plastic at park festivals;
- Purchased rain barrels installed at the Visitor Center and Park Office, maintained wildflower/butterfly gardens, and designated as a Monarch Way Station;
- Upgraded and maintained a public website (*www.graysonfriends.org*) for park and friends information;
- Maintained a weather station and video web cam to provide current weather information via the website;
- Assisted with the Blue Ridge Relay Endurance Race to promote the park and raise funds for projects; and,
- Support special events such as the annual Wayne C. Henderson Music Festival and Guitar Competition and the Annual Fall Harvest Festival.

Friends of High Bridge Trail State Park

Organized: The Friends of High Bridge Trail held their first organizational meeting on February 4, 2009.

Key Organizers: Provisional officers were elected to serve the organization: Sherry Swinson, President; Brian Eckert, Vice President; Woody Ligon, Treasurer; and Ann Ligon, Secretary.

Mission: The Friends support High Bridge Trail through volunteer activities, advocacy, and fundraising.

Projects: The group has volunteered over 1,300 hours. Projects have included:

- Clean-up days, transplanting trees, providing refreshments at programs, sharing park information at events including the Farmville Heart of Virginia Festival and the Appomattox Railroad Festival;
- The Friends played an important role in the park's National Trails Day celebrations, including being a partner for the park's 5K race;
- The Friends received funding from the Friends of Sailor's Creek Battlefield to cover the expense of applying for 501(c)(3) status. In return, the Friends of High Bridge Trail donated funds to the Friends of Bear Creek Lake to cover their expenses for 501(c)(3) application;
- Created an online newsletter and refinished railroad spikes to sell for a fundraiser; and,
- A very significant project of the Friends was a fundraising project called "First to Cross." Partnering with local businesses, the Friends created a contest to select the first person to cross High Bridge at the completion of its restoration. The project raised awareness about the rehabilitation of the bridge and raising funds for the group. The funds raised were used to purchase 70 glass negatives containing images of the 1914 construction of the current High Bridge. The negatives were donated to the park to be preserved and archived.

Friends of Holliday Lake State Park

Organized: Since its inception in 2010, Friends of Holliday Lake members have contributed over 250 volunteer hours and have raised over $2,200 for the park.

Key Organizers: The Friends group currently has four active members and is working to recruit more. Currently, the group is working to achieve the 501(c)(3) status.

Mission: The Friends participate in the mission of the park, which is "to provide opportunities to participate in traditional outdoor recreational activities while appreciating the natural, historical, and cultural resources that are available in and around the Appomattox-Buckingham State Forest in the heart of Virginia."

Projects: Some of Friends activities and efforts, which would otherwise have not been possible, include:

- Raised over $1,000 by hosting the park's first 5K/10K Annual Trail Race sponsored by the park, the Friends, B&W in Lynchburg, and Riverside Runners in Lynchburg;
- Acquired a $1,000 "Keep Virginia Beautiful" grant and to purchased over 500 pocket ashtrays and three smoke urns for use around the park.
- Participated in several special events for the park, including the park's 75th Anniversary Celebration in 2011 and the National Trails Day Celebration in Farmville on June 5, 2010;
- Spent countless hours restoring the butterfly garden at the park, including removing weeds, identifying plants, purchasing plants with their own money, and adding a new hummingbird feeder;
- Designed and promoted FOHLSP fliers for distribution at the park and in the town of Appomattox; and,
- Hiked the Lakeshore Trail to identify the location of downed trees, to assist our maintenance staff.

Friends of Hungry Mother State Park

Organized: In 1998, volunteers began meeting to preserve the beauty of Park Boulevard, which leads to the entrance of Hungry Mother. The group petitioned for Park Boulevard to be designated as a Scenic By-Way. This group transitioned into the Friends of Hungry Mother in 1999, and is continually working to improve and expand conservation efforts.

Key Organizers: John and Judy Taminger, along with other boulevard residents, organized the original group to designate Park Boulevard as a Scenic By-Way.

Mission: The Friends identify and promote activities that conserve and enhance the recreational, cultural, historical, and natural resources of the park and the adjoining highways and by-ways.

Projects: One of the Friends' first projects was obtaining a grant to purchase red bud and dogwood trees to go along Park Boulevard and in the park. The group was also successful in convincing VDOT to plant a flower plot along the Scenic By-Way leading into Hungry Mother State Park. Other projects have included:

- Volunteers staff both the Discovery Center and the Contact Booth. The Friends group has assisted with AmeriCorps, Alternative Spring Break groups, and the Youth Conservation Corps;
- Twice a year the Friends pick up trash. The group also partnered with the park in receiving a grant to purchase solar lights for the park;
- The Friends funded the gazebo where weddings and musical events take place. During the summer months, Saturday nights feature bluegrass and old time music. The Friends help subsidize this weekly favorite; and,
- The group has supported the park's land acquisition interest. In June of 2005, the Hungry Mother Campground, a privately owned campground, became part of Hungry Mother State Park. This purchase added 100 new campsites.

Friends of James River State Park

Organized: The Friends of James River was formed on May 7, 2006, and a positive showing of interested citizens participated. Sam Kerr conducted the meeting, officers were elected, ideas were formed, and the wheels were set in motion. The officers took the group's ideas and have constantly moved forward. The Friends became incorporated in 2006 and a 501(c)(3) nonprofit in March of 2009.

Key Organizers: The Dixon Family, specifically Joanne and Peggy Dixon, along with Judge Sam Kerr were the key organizers. Judge Kerr provided the legal insight for forming the group, and the Dixons provided the legwork and energy to support the initial fundraising activities.

Mission: The Friends act as a nonprofit Citizens Support Organization to assist in conserving the natural, cultural, scenic, and recreational resources of James River State Park; to assist in providing a variety of recreational and educational opportunities; and to assist in promoting environmental stewardship in one of Virginia's most beautiful parks.

Projects: The group has 12 members and has donated over 2,500 volunteer hours. Some projects include:

- The group diligently worked to raise the funds for a new park playground;
- The group is in the beginning stages of a volunteer project known as the Discovery Area, where children can have fun and interact outdoors with natural materials. The construction of the Discovery Area is funded by the Friends group, and all the labor and most materials so far have been donated by volunteers and local businesses; and,
- The Friends are regular sponsors of the annual James River State Park Summer Festival, Fall Festival, and park employee and volunteer recognition events.

Friends of Lake Anna State Park

Organized: The Friends of Lake Anna was organized in 2001.

Key Organizers: Jo W. Finch, President; Kathleen S. Elim, Vice President/Secretary; and Thomas E. Shaw, Treasurer.

Mission: The Friends of Lake Anna State Park actively participate in the mission of the park. That mission is to conserve the natural, cultural, scenic, and recreational resources of the park, as well as to provide a variety of recreational and educational opportunities and to promote environmental stewardship on one of Virginia's largest lakes.

Projects: Since its inception in 2001, Friends of Lake Anna State Park members have contributed over 22,000 hours of volunteer time and over $150,000 in infrastructure improvements at Lake Anna State Park. Examples of these efforts, which would not otherwise been available to park visitors, include:

- Funded Toddler Playground Train and its installation;
- Funded two benches for the playground train area;
- Funded and built 70-seat "classroom in the woods;"
- Funded campfire theater seating;
- Funded two beach spray-off stations and accessible drinking fountain;
- Funded and helped build a new deck at Snack Bar building;
- Purchased a diaper-changing stations for beach bathhouses;
- Purchased a spine board and megaphones for beach safety;
- Created a shoreline erosion control demonstration project;
- Funded, developed, and continue to monitor a bluebird trail in the park;
- Developed a self-guided tour for the Old Pond Trail;
- Funded three fitness stations along the Old Pond Trail; and,
- Funded and completed several landscape projects within the park.

Friends of Leesylvania State Park

Organized: The Friends of Leesylvania had its founding meeting at the Visitor Center the week of when it opened on May 21, 1999. A large group was present along with elected officers.

Key Organizers: Sergeant Major Larry Strickland was a member and staunch supporter of the Friends until his untimely death at the Pentagon on September 11, 2001. The group voted to start a memorial brick area at the Visitor Center where bricks were sold and the money was used by the Friends to support the park. The Recognition Plaza offers park visitors an opportunity to honor friends or family members who have appreciated Leesylvania State Park.

Mission: The Friends actively participate in the Virginia State Park's mission to conserve natural, scenic, historic, and cultural resources of the commonwealth and to provide recreational and educational opportunities consistent with good stewardship of these lands, water, and facilities that leaves them unimpaired for future generations.

Leesylvania State Park

Projects: The Friends assist the park in achieving its goals of serving visitors and protecting Leesylvania's resources through:

- Raising money to provide additional support for programs such as Junior Rangers, free Kids Fishing Tournament, Easter Egg Hunt, C.A.S.T. for Kids, and Haunted History events; and,
- The Friends have made it a point to come to every major function by setting up a table, running programs, sponsoring programs (re-enactors for Lee's of Leesylvania, Civil War Christmas), purchasing needed equipment (computer for the Visitor Center, costumes for re-enacting), and helping with field trips.

Friends of Natural Tunnel State Park

Organized: The 1992 Bond included funding for an environmental ed center at the park. Seeing the need for a foundation, a grassroots movement began. During August of 1998, a fire destroyed the center near its completion. Reconstruction was in question; early members of the Foundation lobbied not to cancel the project. The Cove Ridge Foundation and Advisory Board was officially organized in December 1998. Less than a year later, in August 1999, the Cove Ridge Center was completed. The Cove Ridge Foundation and Advisory Board obtained 501(c)(3) designation in 2005.

Key Organizers: Dr. J.E. Fugate III, Kenny Fannon, Bob McConnell, Isaac Webb, Dan McCoy, Sonny Martin, Chancellor of UVA's College at Wise, President of Mt. Empire Community College, Virginia Meador, Ruby Rogers, Delegate Terry Kilgore, Senator William Wampler Jr., Honorable Ford C. Quillen, Jim Addington, and the Scott County Chamber of Commerce Board.

Mission: The mission is to develop and implement programs, provide organizational structure, and financially support five areas of program concentration: 1) Cultural Arts, 2) Education, 3) Business, 4) Outdoor Pursuits, and 5) Tourism.

Projects: Since its inception, the Foundation has developed many programs. A few include:
- *Virginia Is For Students* Tour and the Nature Trek 360;
- Winter Candlelight Concert Series and Pickin' in the Park events, sponsored by the Cove Ridge Cultural Arts Council;
- Annual Papa Joe Smiddy Mountain Music Festival every Labor Day weekend which is the Foundation's primary fundraiser; and,
- The Foundation has generated funds that have assisted in improvements to park infrastructure and the amphitheater. Over $60,000 has been raised in support.

Friends of Occoneechee State Park

Organized: The Friends of Occoneechee formed in 2008.

Key Organizers: In 2006 several of the park's key community supporters were invited to an organizational meeting to discuss the development of a Friends group for Occoneechee. Many of those who attended this meeting had previously been involved in some capacity as a volunteer or spokesperson for the Park. After two years of additional discussions and finding enough volunteers to assume the role of officers for the group, in the FOOSP was formed in 2008.

Mission: The Friends act as a Citizens Support Organization in assisting to identify and promote activities to conserve, enhance, and interpret the natural, cultural, scenic, historic, educational, and recreational resources of Occoneechee State Park.

Projects: The Friends of Occoneechee serve as volunteers at events and activities, as a nonprofit fund-raising arm for improvements not funded by the state, and to help keep the park and the community in sync. The Friends of Occoneechee State Park have adopted the following projects/events:

- Ongoing Terrace Gardens, Occoneechee Plantation site improvements;
- Ongoing amphitheater improvements;
- Purchase canoes and equipment to expand interpretive program offerings;
- Upgrade lighting at the main boat ramp; and,
- Assist with park special events such as Spring Jazz Fest, Fall Car/Bike Show, and interpretive programming.

Occoneechee Native American Festival

Friends of Pocahontas State Park

Organized: The Friends of Pocahontas was formed in 1996 by citizens who had a strong interest in protecting the park. The Friends became a 501(c)(3) in 2001.

Key Organizers: The initial Friends group was formed by local residents interested in preventing sports complex development at Pocahontas State Park. The Friends group obtained tax exempt status in 2001 with help from Michael Stein.

Mission: The Friends specialize in volunteer assistance to Pocahontas State Park. We shall provide labor and funding for programs and events that are in accordance with the mutual interests of both the Friends of Pocahontas and Pocahontas State Park.

Projects: The Friends group has several park initiatives, including:
- Maintain 14 miles of single track mountain bike trail throughout the park;
- Assist with large events as needed such as the Muddy Buddy, Down and Dirty, and Run Like a Girl race series;
- Split, stock, and sell firewood in the campground as a fund raising initiative;
- Assist with large-scale maintenance projects in the park, such as building painting and cemetery maintenance;
- Sponsor lake and park clean ups and the "Take a Kid Biking" day;
- Work with corporate sponsors such as Wal-Mart, Northrop Grumman, and REI Inc. for supplies, funding, and materials for the park;
- Funded blue bird housing projects;
- Purchased equipment for park use such as a Honda 4 wheel ATV for remote access to trails and a tractor-powered blower to clear trails; and,
- Provided $800-$2,000 annually for Alternative Spring Break groups.

Friends of Sailor's Creek Battlefield Historical State Park Association

Organized: A picnic meeting was held on January 17, 2009, to form a support group. Fourteen volunteers signed up as Friends.

Key Organizers: Greg Eanes, representing a previous support organization, provided a check while the president was instructed to begin the process for incorporation and the filing for 501(c)(3) tax exempt status. Other beginning sizable donations to the group came from the Powhatan Civil War Roundtable and cash donations from a 2008 meeting.

Mission: The Friends of Sailor's Creek Battlefield was formed to act as a nonprofit Citizens Support Organization to assist in conserving the historical, natural, cultural, scenic, and recreational resources of Sailor's Creek Battlefield Historical State Park; to assist in providing a variety of historical, educational, and recreational opportunities; and to assist in promoting environmental stewardship.

Projects: The Friends group relies on donations made by the public at the park's Visitor Center and the Hillsman House. Due to the popularity of battlefield preservation, the group receives sizable contributions. A summary of projects for the park include:
- Purchase of a reproduction Spencer Repeating rifle for demonstrations (private donor);
- Purchase of clothing for living history programs;
- Sponsoring the park's staff to take part in the NPS two-week Black Powder Safety Training program;
- Recasting of a new and accurate National Historic Landmark plaque (private donor);
- Funding of a joint picnic with the High Bridge Friends group;
- Working with Virginia Association for Parks in funding the park's hologram exhibit; and,
- Contributing food and services for the annual Veteran's Day Luminary program.

Friends of Shenandoah River State Park

Organized: In late 2008, the park system asked local residents to form a Friends group to promote the park. The Friends of Shenandoah River was formed in January 2009 with 10 members. It has grown to about 65 members. In mid-2009, the Friends incorporated and received 501(c)(3) exemption.

Key Organizers: The original key organizers included park staff, Dan McDermott, Richard Fox, Brian Bennetta, Virginia Fox, and Mary Bennett.

Mission: To act as a citizen support group; to assist in conserving the natural, cultural, scenic, and recreational resources of Shenandoah River State Park; to assist in providing a variety of recreational and educational opportunities; and to assist in promoting environmental stewardship.

Projects: Friends projects have included:
- Initiate Junior Ranger Day Camp in 2009;
- Create website - *riverparkfriends.org*;
- In 2010, held ParkFest where 14 nonprofits, Audubon Society, Tree Stewards, Trout Unlimited, etc., participated to promote their groups and bring visitors to the park;
- Published a park annual newspaper given to 10,000 visitors;
- In 2011, offered two one-week programs. Thirty campers, ages 7-12, participated in nature and culture programs;
- In 2011, completed a self-guided Junior Ranger program and, with a grant from Kohls Department Stores, a guide was printed;
- Participated in Project Wild training sessions;
- With a grant from the Virginia Bluebird Society, completed construction and installation of 20 new bluebird boxes;
- Landscaped visitor center with native plants;
- Set-up a Virginia State Parks 75th anniversary display at the county library and helped with the anniversary celebration; and,
- Assisted with trail work and programs.

Friends of Sky Meadows State Park

Organized: First organizational meeting held in March 2009 and received 501(c)(3) status in May 2009.

Key Organizers: In early 2009, park management approached long time volunteers Woody Davis, Dori Boulden, and Sean O'Brien to help organize the Friends of Sky Meadows. Woody, Dori, and Sean had been active volunteers at the park for many years, running the "Astronomy for Everyone" program. This trio of dedicated volunteers served as the first executive committee, drafting by-laws, obtaining tax exempt status, and growing the membership.

Mission: The mission of the Friends of Sky Meadows is to assist with identifying and promoting activities to conserve, enhance, and interpret cultural, scenic, recreational and historic resources of Sky Meadows State Park; to assist in providing a variety of recreational, and educational opportunities; and to assist in promoting the stewardship and funding needs of Sky Meadows State Park, Virginia State Parks, and the Virginia Association for Parks.

Projects: Since its inception, the Friends have contributed 2,345 volunteer hours and funded projects totaling $2,000, including:

- *"Second Saturday Kids' Craft"* program, covered the materials costs and provided a volunteer;
- Established an Environmental Educator Scholarship fund, enabling interested park volunteers and Master Naturalists to attend the DEQ's Watershed Educator Institute;
- Co-sponsored the Great American Backyard Campout, the 75th Anniversary Celebration, and the 2011 Fall Farm Festival;
- Helped cover the Virginia State Park booth at the Virginia Scottish Games and the RV Expo; and,
- Assisted with the January 2010 VAFP meeting, funded two volunteer recognition events, and funded park staff training in volunteer management.

Friends of Smith Mountain Lake State Park

Organized: On April 30, 1996, Virginia gained its first official state park Friends group. By July 1996, the Articles of Incorporation were completed and the Friends of Smith Mountain Lake State Park became a 501(c)(3) nonprofit.

Key Organizers: During the mid 1990's, several areas of the park were facing a shutdown in the off season. The staff approached volunteer Ray Haymaker to develop a group of people to assist the park in helping keep areas of the park open to the public. Currently the 77 Friends members are involved in many projects.

Mission: The Friends endeavor to be good stewards of Smith Mountain Lake State Park through programs and projects.

Projects: Through the years, members have participated in programs to better serve the park. These have included:

- The successful Spring Fling Festival of arts, crafts, food, and music, attracting over 5,000 visitors;
- Assisting in the formation of Friends groups at other parks;
- Collaborating to establish an osprey nest in the park with a live camera to follow the progression of offspring;
- Staffing the Discovery Center during the summer months;
- Maintaining a butterfly and native species garden surrounding the Discovery Center;
- Assisting with interpretive programs, operating the hay wagon, organizing Music in the Park, conducting a children's fishing tournament, offering a Winter Lecture Series, and continually cleaning up park trails;
- Developing a reading program for the hundreds of children staying at the park during the summer;
- Working on nesting boxes programs for bluebirds, wood ducks, and purple martin habitat; and,
- In addition, the Friends are members of VAFP and give support to this group.

Friends of Southwest Virginia Museum Historical State Park

Organized: The first Friends meeting was in October of 2005 and the group officially organized in December. The Friends are a 501 (c)(3) nonprofit. In addition to the Friends group, the site is benefited from, and advocated for, by the C. Bascom Slemp Foundation.

Key Organizers: Organizing members included Norma Sieman, Dr. Lawrence Fleenor, Rebecca Stapleton, Deborah Wright, C.F. Wright, Jettie Hess, Carol Moore, and Garnett Gilliam. The Friends also organized junior memberships for teens which is unique to the Friends of the Museum.

Mission: The mission of the Friends is to act as a Citizens Support Organization in assisting to identify and promote activities to conserve, enhance, and interpret the cultural and historic resources of the Southwest Virginia Museum.

Projects: Annually the Friends contribute over $40,000 in support with hundreds of volunteer hours. Some projects include:
- Started the "Gathering In The Gap" Roots Music Festival in 2007, which has featured such artists as Marty Stuart, Darrell Scott, John Carter Cash, Blue Highway, and other esteemed musicians;
- Assist with programming including the Festival of Trees, Hoots and Haints Halloween event, Coffee House, Lunch on the Lawn, 9-11 Day of Service, and various fundraising events;
- Purchase numerous equipment and supplies for the site including tables, chairs, kitchen equipment, landscaping, scanner, food for programs, and more;
- Maintain the Friends' website (*swvamuseum.org*) and the festival website (*gatheringinthegapmusicfestival.com*); and,
- Advocate on issues that affect the Southwest Virginia Museum Historical State Park and the Virginia State Park system.

Friends of Staunton River Battlefield State Park

Organized: The Friends group, the Historic Staunton River Foundation, is a volunteer-based, nonprofit, organization that was formed in 1994.

Key Organizers: The Foundation is membership driven and relies solely on the support and dedication of a volunteer staff. The governing body of the Foundation is its 17 member Board of Trustees.

Mission: The Foundation exists with the scope and purpose of promoting, developing, and preserving the 1864 Battlefield at the Staunton River; the Staunton River Bridge; the Staunton River historical areas and environs; the Roanoke Station; Mulberry Hill Plantation, the ancestral home of the Carrington family; 44CH62, the Randy K. Wade Archaeological Site and any future archaeological discoveries in the area along the Staunton River; and the Sappony Indian Nation.

Staunton River Battlefield

Projects: Foundation projects include:
- Collecting artifacts for display and preserving the integrity of the Staunton River environs and archaeological sites;
- Providing historical, environmental, wildlife, and wetlands education as well as assisting in developing programs and events for the general public at the Staunton River Battlefield; and,
- Sponsoring the Easter Egg Hunt, the highly attended June Commemoration of the Battle, wagon rides, interpretive programs and workshops, canoe rides, nature walks, Haunted Harvest Hayride, and hosting an Antebellum Christmas Open House at Mulberry Hill.

Friends of Westmoreland State Park

Organized: The Friends of Westmoreland held their organizational meeting in March 2011 at the park's historic Civilian Conservation Corps' built hall.

Mission: The mission of the Friends is to act as a Citizens Support Organization in assisting to identify and promote activities to conserve, enhance, and interpret the resources of Westmoreland State Park, one of the six original Virginia State Parks.

Restored CCC Fountain at Westmoreland State Park

Projects: The Friends of Westmoreland's projects:
- First major undertaking was the renovation of a CCC built fountain in the park. The staff and Friends worked together to dig and remove all the dirt that had occupied the former fountain space. Contractors were brought in to do some stone work and seal the fountain. On the 75th Anniversary, the fountain came to life as a 1936 Buffalo nickel was tossed into the running wishing well; and,
- Additionally, the Friends participated in the Westmoreland Winter Open House and First Day Hike held in January of each year. The Friends are looking forward to many years of supporting and serving Westmoreland State Park.

Friends of Wilderness Road State Park

Organized: The Friends of Wilderness Road organized in 1997.

Key Organizers: Charles Allen, Freda Ayers, Sue Beaty, Ron Caldwell, Tom Coker, Sue Crockett, Jason and Martha Davis, Garry Ely, Terry Esteys, Victor Harbor, Hunter Hensley, Robbie Hines, Jim Hopkins, Patsy Houck, Lois Hounshell-Rogers, France Inwood, Sheila Kuczho, Ralph Miner, Kyle and Sue Rosenbalm, Ora Rowlette, Betty and Bob Smith, James Sutphin, and Shirley and Don Watson.

Mission: The Friends consist of citizens, businesses, civic groups, and students dedicated to the continuing development of Wilderness Road State Park. The goals are to:
- Support and promote the park's projects;
- Seek financial support from a variety of sources: fundraising on site, in-kind contributions, donation of goods and services, and sales revenue and membership dues; and,
- Seek local community support from organizations, groups, and individuals by sponsoring events, workshops, etc. that help educate the public about the Park. Facilitate communication between the local community and park staff.

Projects: The Friends of Wilderness Road, through monetary support and volunteer hours, has contributed to the following:
- Visitors Center-dedicated in October 2004-has interpretive exhibits, a gift shop, and a theater;
- Picnic areas, three shelters, and an outdoor comfort station;
- Indian Ridge Trail, Karlan mansion, furniture, and computer;
- Wilderness Road Trail connecting the Park to the Cumberland Gap National Historical Park and providing opportunities for hiking, biking, and horseback riding;
- Children's playground;
- Grounds maintenance;
- Park development projects using grant monies; and
- Help sponsor Easter at Karlan, The Raid on Martin's Station, Pumpkins in the Park, dinner theater, and Christmas at Karlan Mansion.

Friends of York River State Park

Organized: The Friends of York River was founded in 1994.

Key Organizers: Original President Connie Holland, Vice President Ann Lipp, Secretary Joyce Ferguson, and Treasurer Alberta Gossett. 2012 President Cynthia Kozak, Vice President Penny Rich, Secretary Sharon Stanley, and Treasurer Vivian Carpenter.

Mission: The Friends provide volunteer nonprofit assistance to the Department of Conservation and Recreation for the continued preservation of York River State Park by supplying funds, materials, and/or labor for projects and provide education to the community about the park.

Projects: Some of the Friends projects include:
- Establishing playgrounds;
- Donating visitors center display cases;
- Maintaining the Wild Plant Arboretum;
- Sponsoring the Saltwater Fishing Tournament and 5K Race;
- Maintaining the mountain bike trails with the Eastern Virginia Mountain Bike Association;
- Maintaining a website highlighting the archaeological significance of Taskinas Plantation;
- Aiding with cleanup after Hurricane Irene;
- Contributing over 2,000 volunteer hours per year and more than $25,000 in park improvement projects and programs in the last five years;
- Established Youth in Nature Scholarship Fund, accessible slide for canoe launch, park trail and gardens maintenance and upgrades, and;
- In 2012, the Friends placed a special emphasis on activities that immerse youth in nature. They assisted the Virginia State Parks Youth Conservation Corps program and helped fund scholarships for area young adults involved in outdoor activities and preservation.

Volunteers plant a tree at Mason Neck State Park

Virginia Association for Parks members at the General Assembly Building with the Virginia State Parks Booth

Volunteers from Dominion work with Friends of Lake Anna State Park on shoreline erosion project

VAFP and
Virginia National Parks

As discussed previously, VAFP encountered difficulty with the NPS organizational structure because parts of the Commonwealth fall into three different NPS regions. Similarly, Virginia's US Congressional delegation represents a very small percentage of the total votes in Congress, making it difficult for VAFP to have a significant legislative impact from a national perspective.

Notwithstanding these impediments, VAFP has worked diligently each year for the NPS cause. As of 2012, Lynn Davis serves as the Chair for National Parks and was instrumental in organizing VAFP from its inception. Each year, VAFP has sent letters to members of the Virginia Congressional delegation, as well as to the chairs of the pertinent committees and subcommittees, encouraging support for NPS' budget and for increased appropriations to the Land and Water Conservation Fund. VAFP also adopted the strategy of supporting various initiatives launched by the National Parks Conservation Association.

National Parks Friends Show Support:
Friends Groups' Histories

National Park Friends groups are a significant, growing source of financial and volunteer support. According to the 2010 National Park Foundation report, there has been a significant spike in the number of Friends groups since they first started in 1919: 26% of all Friends groups were established only in the last 10 years. 96% of Friends roups are registered as 501(c)(3) organizations and 85% have some type of formal agreement with NPS. However, most Friends groups are all volunteer-run, and 75% have an annual budget of less than $500,000. Following are the NPS recognized Friends groups. The first three descriptions were provided by the individual friends group while the following descriptions were obtained from the National Park Service. VAFP: Forging The Path 82

Friends groups in National Parks help the various sites in many ways, such as building wildlife viewing platforms

Friends of Historic Green Spring hold an open house for the public

Volunteers help the Friends of the Blue Ridge Parkway

Friends of Blue Ridge Parkway

Organized: The Friends of the Blue Ridge Parkway was organized in June 1988.

Key Organizers: Jack Smith, Roanoke Chamber of Commerce, served as chairman of a citizens' committee on the 50th Anniversary Celebration of the Blue Ridge Parkway. Then Parkway Superintendent Gary Everhardt asked Smith to form a Friends group to support parkway efforts and needs. Mary Guynn of Galax, Virginia, was one of the founding members. She continues serving today as Board Emeritus. Lynn Davis assisted in spearheading the nonprofit organization. After Smith died, Lynn served as interim director from 1990-1992 and has continued to serve on the Friends Board of Directors.

Mission: The Friends mission is to help preserve, promote and enhance the outstanding natural beauty, ecological vitality and cultural distinctiveness of the Blue Ridge Parkway and its surrounding scenic landscape, thereby preserving this national treasure for future generations.

Projects: With over 9,000 members, the Friends work to save parkway views and vistas, recruit volunteers, secure trails and preserve historical structures. The Friends fund planting of parkway view sheds, interpretive exhibits, environmental education programs, hemlock research, and much more, all to empower individual responsibility in the preservation and protection of this unique natural resource, the Blue Ridge Parkway. The Friends *Next Generation of Stewards* program reconnects kids with nature. This program promotes outdoor volunteer opportunities and Junior Ranger Programs. For every $1 donated to the Friends, $3 is leveraged in volunteer service on the parkway. Over $1,000,000 is provided by parkway volunteers annually.   Working with the Parkway border communities, the Friends make a difference to both preserve the parkway and to provide volunteers and funding for parkway projects.

Friends of Booker T. Washington National Monument

Organized: The first organizational meeting was in February 2008. It incorporated with the IRS in June 2008.

Key Organizers: Long before Booker T. Washington had an official Friends group, the park had active volunteers who gave numerous hours to the park in gardening, tending farm animals, ensuring water quality, and supporting park signature events. In January 2008, Superintendent Rebecca Harriet, asked a group of passionate volunteers to form the Friends group. The founding members were Penny Blue, Lillie Head, Wilbert Head, Jean Hines, Lonnie Hines, Sue Joyce, Don Kelso, Sandy Kelso, George McLaughlin, Linda McLaughlin, John Tully, and Kathleen Tully. After several months of planning, the Friends signed the NPS partnership agreement. Both Nancy Woods, from the NPS Northeast Region Office of Park Partnerships, and Cynthia Morris, Director of the African American Experience Fund, were able to join the Friends for the signing.

Mission: The Friends support Booker T. Washington National Monument and its mission to preserve and protect the birth site and childhood home of Booker T. Washington and promote public awareness and appreciation for his legacy.

Projects: The Friends received a $10,000 start-up grant from the African American Experience Fund. The Friends have since obtained a number of grants and now are able to provide financial support and countless volunteer hours to support the Park's signature events such as Juneteenth and Harvest Festival; newly formed groups, like the Living History Guild and the Research Institute; and ongoing activities such as visitor services, farming, maintaining the heirloom garden, natural resource management and a community garden. The Friends held its first major fundraising event which celebrated Mr. Washington's Birthday.

Potomac Appalachian Trail Club (PATC) Partnership with Shenandoah National Park

Organized: The Potomac Appalachian Trail Club (PATC) was established in November 1927 to help build the Appalachian Trail in the Mid-Atlantic region. The PATC is a nonprofit, volunteer, membership club of the Appalachian Trail Conservancy.

Key Organizers: The PATC was organized by a group of eight visionaries in 1927 and has grown to more than 6,500 members. Activities are led by volunteer committee chairs, with chairs serving on the PATC Council. An Executive Committee, elected by the general membership and consisting of 11 members, is responsible for executing the policies of Council. The Club's organizers also include several appointed officers and paid staff members.

Mission: The PATC, through volunteer efforts, education, and advocacy, maintains and protects the Appalachian Trail and nearby lands as well as acquires and maintains other trails and related facilities in the Mid-Atlantic region for the enjoyment of present and future hikers.

Projects and Programs: The PATC and park have joined in trail stewardship since the park's establishment in 1936. In 2011, PATC contributed over 27,000 volunteer hours. The group maintains and operates the park's backcountry structures, six cabins and 11 AT historic hut facilities, with AT Ridgerunner and trail patrol programs to assist backcountry visitors. PATC's Shenandoah Mountain Rescue Group conducts search and rescue training cooperatively with Park staff. Other programs include educate visitors in *Leave No Trace*, conduct outreach outdoor education programs, and observe and report on backcountry conditions. PATC also supports the Park in securing public access at boundary trailheads by providing funding and lands planning personnel to accomplish lands protection on the park boundary.

Appalachian National Scenic Trail

Friends Group: Appalachian Trail Conservancy

Mission: To preserve and manage the Appalachian Trail ensuring that its vast natural beauty and priceless cultural heritage can be shared and enjoyed today, tomorrow, and for centuries to come.

Appomattox Court House National Historical Park

McClean House at Appomattox

Friends Group: Appomattox 1865 Foundation

Mission: The mission of the Appomattox 1865 Foundation is to enrich the understanding and appreciation of the heritage and significance of Appomattox Court House National Historical Park. The foundation focuses on education efforts to preserve the past, augment support, commemorate history, and enhance the visitor's experience at the park.

Arlington House, The Robert E. Lee Memorial

Friends Group: Save Historic Arlington House Incorporated

Mission: To promote the restoration, preservation, and advancement of research and educational activities relative to the historic home of George Washington Parke Custis and Robert E. Lee (the "Arlington House"), to assist the National Park Service's stewardship of the Arlington House, and to assist with the restoration and maintenance of the building and its grounds.

Assateague Island National Seashore

Friends Groups: Assateague Island Alliance and Assateague Coastal Trust

Mission: Assateague Island Alliance was created to benefit Assateague Island National Seashore by supporting interpretive, educational, and scientific programs; ensuring stewardship, restoration, and preservation of our land, water, living resources, and historical sites; and balancing high quality resource-compatible recreation.

Assateague Coastal Trust works to protect and enhance the natural resources of the Atlantic Coastal Bays watershed through advocacy, conservation and education.

Claude Moore Colonial Farm

Friends Group: Friends of Claude Moore Colonial Farm

Mission: To support and operate the only privately operated National Park in the United States and to educate the public about American agriculture through active participation and involvement in an 18th century low-income family farm and its related programs.

Colonial National Historical Park: Green Springs National Historic Landmark District

Friends Group: The Friends of the National Park Service for Greens Springs Incorporated.

Mission: To research, preserve, and present Historic Green Springs and its history for public education and enjoyment.

Cumberland Gap National Historical Park

Friends Group: Friends of Cumberland Gap National Historical Park Incorporated

Mission: To strengthen awareness and assist the NPS in its mission to preserve, protect, and enhance the natural and cultural resources of Cumberland Gap National Historical Park by providing community education, wellness, opportunities, expertise, advocacy, and inspiration for the park through fundraising efforts and volunteering.

White Rocks at Cumberland Gap National Historical Park

Dyke Marsh

Friends Group: Friends of Dyke Marsh Incorporated

Mission: To monitor and protect the marsh and its flora and fauna by working in cooperation with the citizenry, the local governments, and the National Park Service.

Lynn Davis, VAFP Chair for National Parks, speaks at the 2011 Spring Conference at Smith Mountain Lake State Park

Fredericksburg and Spotsylvania National Military Parks

Friends Group(s): Friends of Fredericksburg Area Battlefields (FoFAB) and Friends of Wilderness Battlefield (FoWB)

Mission: Founded in 1997, FoFAB is a nonprofit, tax exempt Civil War preservation organization dedicated to providing educational programs, advocacy, fundraising, and service projects for the preservation of both National Park Service lands and privately owned battlefield property in the Fredericksburg, Virginia, area where numerous Civil War battles took place.

The purpose of the Friends of Wilderness Battlefield (FoWB) is to assist the Fredericksburg and Spotsylvania National Military Park in its efforts to preserve the Wilderness Battlefield in Spotsylvania and Orange Counties. The Friends provide advocacy, educational programs, and service projects.

Maggie L. Walker National Historical Site

Friends Group: Maggie L. Walker Historical Foundation

Mission: To perpetuate the life and legacy of Maggie L. Walker

Manassas National Battlefield Park

Friends Group: Friends of Manassas National Battlefield Park

Mission: To support the Manassas National Battlefield Park and preserve the Park's historic significance and cultural and natural resources, to encourage community involvement and volunteerism in the Park, to provide a forum for community outreach, and to promote educational and cultural programs.

Overmountain Victory National Historic Trail

Friends Group: Overmountain Victory Trail Association

Mission: Through education, preservation and interpretation, its mission is to protect, preserve and interpret the route of the Campaign to the Battle of Kings Mountain.

Shenandoah National Park

Friends Group: Shenandoah National Park Trust

Fall in White Oak Canyon, Shenandoah National Park

Mission: Shenandoah National Park Trust helps protect and enhance Shenandoah National Park for current visitors and future generations. The Trust is the official nonprofit fundraising partner for Shenandoah National Park. The Trust collaborates with the park superintendent and staff to identify priority projects that government funding will not cover.

Prince William Forest Park

Friends Group: Friends of Prince William Forest Park

Mission: To advocate for the preservation and enhancement of the natural and cultural resources of Prince William Forest Park, a unit of the National Park Service, in Triangle, Virginia.

Wolf Trap National Park for the Performing Arts

Friends Group: Wolf Trap Foundation for the Performing Arts

Mission: To present and create excellent and innovative performing arts programs for the enrichment, education, and enjoyment of diverse audiences and participants.

"Yesterday-Today-Tomorrow"

The intent of this document is twofold – to celebrate VAFP's first 15 years of organizational history and to provide specific examples of what a group of thoughtful, committed citizens can do when they voluntarily take on issues of interest. It is hoped that this document will both encourage and be useful to other citizen groups in Virginia, and perhaps in other states, as they form to address their respective areas of interest.

From the volunteers' perspective, the Virginia Association for Parks' first 15 years has been both a labor of love and an exhilarating ride! We look back on those first 15 years with great pride and look forward to our next 15 years with eager anticipation.

"Yesterday. Today. Tomorrow. Virginians Love their Parks!"

Jo Finch - Secretary, VAFP, Jim Klakowicz - State Parks Chair, VAFP, Ann Lipp - Treasurer, VAFP, Johnny Finch - President, VAFP, Senator Emmett Hanger - Legislator of the Year 2008, Joe Elton - Director, Virginia State Parks, Jim Dillard - 2003 Legislator of the Year

19194338R00051

Made in the USA
Charleston, SC
11 May 2013